Common Plants
of the Mid-Atlantic Coast

Gene M. Silberhorn is a senior marine scientist and associate professor at the Virginia Institute of Marine Science, School of Marine Science, College of William and Mary. Mary Warinner holds a bachelor's degree in fine arts and biology and a master's degree in landscape architecture, both from the University of Virginia. They previously collaborated on another book, *Wetland Plants of Virginia*.

Common Plants of the Mid-Atlantic Coast

A Field Guide

Gene M. Silberhorn

Illustrations by Mary Warinner

THE JOHNS HOPKINS UNIVERSITY PRESS
Baltimore and London

The Johns Hopkins University Press, Baltimore, Maryland 21218
The Johns Hopkins Press Ltd., London

Library of Congress Cataloging in Publication Data

Silberhorn, Gene M.
    Common plants of the mid-Atlantic coast.

    Bibliography: pp. 251–54
    Includes index.
    1. Coastal flora — Middle Atlantic States — Identification.
    2. Botany — Middle Atlantic States.
I. Warinner, Mary.   II. Title.
QK122.5.S54   581.975   81–48177
ISBN 0–8018–2319–6   AACR2
ISBN 0–8018–2725–6 (pbk.)

To Sue, Mike, and Dave

Contents

Preface

This field guide was written for those who want to know more about the common plants of the Mid-Atlantic coastal region. This coastal zone, which extends from Long Island, New York, to Cape Fear, North Carolina, is known to mariners and oceanographers as the Mid-Atlantic Bight. The Atlantic shoreline segment that extends from Cape Cod to Cape Hatteras forms a shallow curve or bight. Within this physiographic zone a wide variety of coastal and marine flora and fauna are found. A number of southern and northern animal species migrate and converge here. The southern and northern range limits of a number of coastal plant species are also found and overlap in this zone. Hence the area is an interesting one for amateur and professional naturalists alike.

A glossary is included for the reader's convenience. Though an attempt was made to avoid burdensome terminology, some of the more important and interesting plant characteristics necessitate explanation in basic botanical terms. In many cases, technical language is explained in the text.

The fine drawings by Mary Warinner are a most important feature of this publication. Most of the plants were drawn from living specimens. Nearly all species are depicted with fruits or flowers or both.

This volume should not, of course, be considered a treatise or monograph. Many plant species found in the Mid-Atlantic coastal region are not treated in this book. Effort was made, rather, to include those that are either typical, common, abundant, or endemic. More than a few plants in this book fit all of these categories.

Acknowledgments

I wish to thank the Virginia Institute of Marine Science, School of Marine Science, College of William and Mary for the financial support that made this book possible.

I also am grateful to Dr. Michael Bender, Mr. Fred Biggs, Dr. William Hargis, Jr., and Mr. Paul Koehly for their help and encouragement.

Thanks also go to Mr. Joseph Gilley and Mrs. Kay Stubblefield for graphics.

For critical readings during various stages of manuscript development, I am indebted to Dr. Jesse Clovis, Mr. Richard Cook, Ms. Marti Germann, Ms. Mary Jane Lewis, Dr. William Niering, and Dr. Stanwyn Shetler.

I also appreciate the effort of Mrs. Nancy White in typing the initial stages of the manuscript.

Special thanks go to the staff of the Johns Hopkins University Press for helpful suggestions and especially to Mr. Anders Richter who kept the momentum going.

Finally, I thank colleagues, co-workers and students who accompanied me in the field on numerous occasions throughout the Mid-Atlantic Coast.

Common Plants
of the Mid-Atlantic Coast

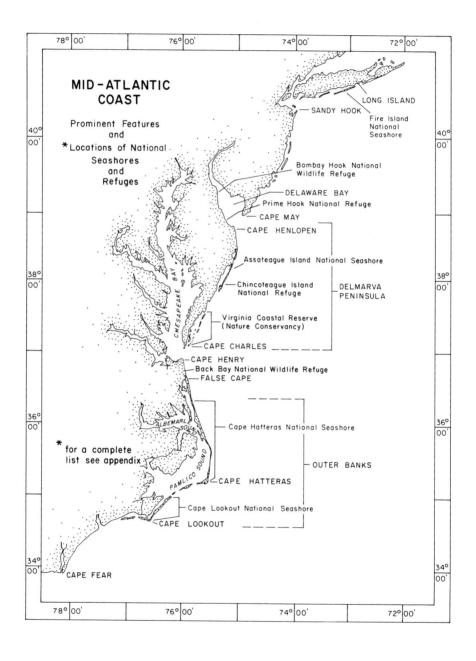

MID-ATLANTIC COAST

Prominent Features
and
*Locations of National
Seashores
and
Refuges

LONG ISLAND
SANDY HOOK
Fire Island
National
Seashore

Bombay Hook National
Wildlife Refuge
DELAWARE BAY
Prime Hook National Refuge
CAPE MAY
CAPE HENLOPEN

Assateague Island National Seashore

Chincoteague Island
National Refuge
DELMARVA
PENINSULA

Virginia Coastal Reserve
(Nature Conservancy)
CAPE CHARLES

CAPE HENRY
Back Bay National Wildlife Refuge
FALSE CAPE

CHESAPEAKE BAY

ALBEMARLE
SOUND
Cape Hatteras National Seashore

* for a complete
list see appendix

OUTER BANKS

PAMLICO SOUND
CAPE HATTERAS

Cape Lookout National Seashore
CAPE LOOKOUT

CAPE FEAR

78° 00'   76° 00'   74° 00'   72° 00'
40° 00'
38° 00'
36° 00'
34° 00'

Introduction

The seacoast has held great appeal for man and has inspired a rich body of lore throughout the ages. It has provided shelter for his vessels, food for his table, and salt to season it. Its protected estuaries have been developed and dredged to accommodate maritime commerce. Its aquatic fauna is harvested for its staple quantity and epicurean quality. Contiguous bays, lagoons, sounds, and marshes are magnetic not only for waterfowl but for birdwatchers and hunters as well.

The sand of its beaches is a special commodity in warm sunny weather, but its residues are brushed away as one departs. Beach-combers seek the bounty that rolls and tumbles on the glistening, mobile interface with the sea or that lies half-buried within it. Shore-birds nest on the sand, disguised and protected by a ridiculous trifle of flotsam and withered grass.

There are those who stand with great anticipation grasping a fiber-glass rod, eager for it to become suddenly alive. Others are more relaxed, standing or sitting, some fishing, some not, mesmerized, their backs to the world they left behind. Then there are those of freer spirit, whose attraction is more physical and who are perhaps more cognizant of the power generated by the sea. They rest on boards, not too far out, talking and joking until one of them shouts. Heads turn. Judgments are made. They propell themselves frantically with their hands. If prowess prevails they experience the thrust and power of the surf in a continuous, exhilarating motion to the shoreline, where different worlds meet, clash, and fall away from each other.

The most attractive and popular appeal of the coastal zone is the beach. It is, after all, the most dynamic of its wonders. But there is more to a beach than boardwalks, hotels, condominiums, discos, bars, seafood restaurants, hot dog stands, and parking lots. Some of the least populated, cleanest, widest, and most esthetically pleasing beaches are those devoid of the above trappings. In federal, state, and local parks and refuges throughout the Mid-Atlantic region one can explore not only the beach but the fore dunes and the dune fields behind them. One can note what lies exposed in the blowouts, perhaps artifacts of an earlier time. One can sample a ripe Beach Plum or follow animal tracks into the cool of the maritime forest. One can traverse the forest and break into a vista of a prairie-like marsh that grades ever so gently into the sound.

Undeveloped coastal areas typically support plants that have adapted to the harsh environment. Some adaptive features are obvious, others are not. Some species are easily recognized yet appear different from their inland relatives. Some plants lend a desert-like motif, and still others appear insignificant, growing as if in desperation on hot white sand. Some grasses grow in full exposure on the very tops of primary dunes, in open defiance of salt spray, gale-force winds, and drifting sand.

These species are heavily stressed by the natural environment, likely to their limit of tolerance. If dune plants are further impacted by man, carelessly walking or driving over them, they usually die in a short period of time. Repeated disturbance almost always results in rutted, compacted sand and mutilated vegetation. These areas are the first to erode during bouts of high wind, pelting rain, and storm-driven surf. Visitors to seashore parks and refuges are hence reminded to keep off the dunes except in areas where boardwalks and similar structures are provided. Dune vegetation is critical to the integrity of the dune system. The flexible stems and leaves of dune plants act as wind buffers, reducing wind velocity and its impact on the dunes. The root and rhizome systems of dune grasses are effective sand binders. The primary dune complex itself is a barrier to storms, protecting the interior areas of the coastal system.

There are many threats to the stability of the Mid-Atlantic Coast. Along with storms and hurricanes, man, through poorly planned development, has contributed more than his share of destruction. In many areas, the protective primary dunes have been leveled to accommodate beach homes, hotels, condominiums, and the like. The primary dunes adjacent to the beach receive the brunt of storm-generated waves and surges. When dunes are no longer there to serve as buffers, it is the buildings that suffer the ravages of storms.

Having recognized the fragility and protective nature of the primary dunes and their stabilizing vegetation, a number of states along the Atlantic Coast have enacted protective laws. While the nature of these laws varies greatly from state to state, they nonetheless demonstrate that concerned citizens are recognizing the need for management. Until recently, much development was done with little or no regard for the environment or for safeguards for people or property. While newly enacted laws have provided guidelines for better management methods, some coastal communities are experiencing severe erosional problems from even minor storms.

Short-term catastrophic events such as hurricanes and violent nor'easters are a real threat as well. The Mid-Atlantic Bight has been mercifully spared in the last few years, but to expect the hiatus to continue is foolhardy. Over the years hurricanes and storms are forgotten, but memories are painful for those who have experienced their fury. Recently, I had sobering reminder of the destructive power of hurricanes while studying two series of more than a hundred aerial photographs taken in 1938 and 1960 of the entire thirty-two–mile length of Fire Island, a narrow barrier island off the southern coast of Long Island. Both series were taken within a day or two after major hurricanes struck the New Jersey and New York coasts. The more destructive storm was the New England or Long Island Express hurricane of 1938. The other was the infamous Donna of 1960. Acres of debris littered the dunes and flats. Much of the wreckage was beach homes broken and tumbled together as if they were toy blocks, hundreds of feet from their foundations and pilings. Massive overwash fans reached nearly to Great South Bay. Though the storms occurred twenty-two years apart, in many areas they invaded the coast in the same places, that is, those sites where the primary dunes were low or nonexistent. Some of these overwash areas are now densely developed while others are vegetated by coastal plant communities. Even though large areas of the coast have been developed, broad expanses of coastal vegetation prevail within Fire Island National Seashore and in national seashores, refuges, and parks all along the Mid-Atlantic Coast.

For the most part, the Mid-Atlantic Coast has three shorelines rather than just one. The bounding surf of the Atlantic is the most dynamic. This, of course, is the ocean side or outer shoreline of the barrier islands and barrier beaches that are strung along much of the Mid-Atlantic Coast. These narrow strips of sand are evident even on satellite imagery. From more than 250 miles above the Earth, astronauts commented on the glistening white beaches, which seems incredible given that barrier islands and beaches are seldom more than a mile wide.

Barrier islands are essentially long (2 to 30 miles or more) narrow strips of sand that lie a few hundred yards up to more than a mile off the mainland and are several hundred yards to no more than a mile and a half wide. The main components of a barrier island are the ocean beach, dunes (which may or may not be vegetated), and a marsh system on the landward side. Shrub communities and sometimes maritime forests are also parts of the system. Barrier beaches are essentially barrier islands connected to the mainland at one end or perhaps at several places.

Therefore, there are effectively three shorelines: the ocean shoreline, active and characterized by broad, open, sand beaches; the sound side (landward side of the barrier island or beach), which may be fringed with marsh or perhaps with large expanses of it; and the mainland shoreline, which may have sandy beaches (perhaps less extensive than the ocean beach), or marshes, or if developed, seawalls, bulkheads, or the like.

In certain areas along the Atlantic Coast, barrier islands and barrier beaches are migrating westward towards the mainland because of a general rise in sea level. Polar ice melt over thousands of years is one of the main reasons for the increase in sea level. Ice melt and land subsidence (sinking) in certain areas are critical factors that must be considered in long-range planning and management. Subsidence, caused by various geological processes, may be further complicated by long-term groundwater withdrawal.

Some of the most productive ecosystems in the world are found behind barrier islands and barrier beaches. Salt marshes, algae-rich tidal flats, and shallow-water sea grass beds are parts of the bay and lagoon system that lies between these coastal formations and the mainland.

Salt marshes dominated by Saltmarsh Cordgrass are found along the coast from Maine to Texas. On the Atlantic Coast, these prairie-like wetlands are the most highly developed in South Carolina and Georgia where vigorous grassy wetlands extend for miles. In the Mid-Atlantic Bight region, the most extensive undeveloped saltmarshes are found from the New Jersey coast to North Carolina. In most areas, Saltmarsh Cordgrass grows in the intertidal zone, primarily between sea level and mean high water. This is one of the more severe environments that vascular plants encounter. Tidal flooding is particularly harsh on developing sprigs of Cordgrass. During high tide they are usually submerged in water turbid with suspended sediment: sunlight is restricted, photosynthesis is reduced, and plant growth is affected. Although marsh peat and Cordgrass are resistant to storm-lashed waves, erosion takes its toll in many marshes. Saltmarsh Cordgrass must also overcome sea strength salinity of 3.5 percent. This grass has unique morphological mechanisms and a complex physiology that counteracts high salinity. However, if other factors enter the ecosystem, such as various types of pollution or dredged spoil deposition, the population may not be able to survive because normal stress factors may already have pushed its tolerance levels to the limit.

Despite real and potential stress factors, salt marshes produce a quantity of vegetative matter that rivals the production statistics of wheat, corn, and even sugar cane — all without the benefit of cultivation, fertilization, or pesticides. About half of the plant material produced in a salt marsh is flushed into a system of channels, creeks, and guts. Here this material, known as detritus, is decomposed by marine bacteria and fungi into small particles. Saline marshes in the Mid-Atlantic region produce between three and six tons of detritus per acre per year. Microscopic crustaceans (copepods and amphipods) feed upon the bacteria and fungi. Minnows, juvenile fish, and other fish such as menhaden consume these crustaceans by the multitude. Crabs, oysters, and clams filter-feed upon the particles suspended in the water column. Larger fish, such as flounder, weak fish (gray trout), blue fish, and striped bass, prey upon the smaller fish. Importantly, nearly 90 percent of commercial and sport fish on the Atlantic Coast are dependent upon the byproducts of salt marshes.

The other half of the detritus stays within the marsh system. This organic material, along with sediments, forms marsh peat. Peat is the substrate upon which the marsh grows. The top eight to ten inches of it are densely interlaced with stout rhizomes (underground stems) and roots of Saltmarsh Cordgrass stands. This mixture of living and partially decayed plant material is tough and permeable, valuable attributes in an aquatic marine system. Marsh peat generally accumulates at a rate of approximately one foot per century. Some marsh peat in the Mid-Atlantic region is between 35 and 45 feet deep, or 3,500 to 4,500 years old. Despite the gradual rise in sea level, the marsh maintains its existence as a viable ecological system.

The high productivity of a marsh can, however, be a problem. Strong westerly winds and weak easterlys and nor'easters during the winter months can cause a buildup of detritus behind the barrier islands. Huge rafts of plant material become lodged on the marsh, and through compaction, shading, and other factors, such rafts can smother and kill the plant life.

Sand overwash, caused by high intensity storms breaking through or around the protective dunes, often reaches the marsh and covers it to depths that Saltmarsh Cordgrass cannot recover from. Overwash, however, it not always detrimental. A thin veneer adds sediment and nutrients to the system.

The most destructive force that impacts wetlands is man. Until recent years, marshes were greatly exploited. They were dredged to facilitate boat access and filled to accommodate development. They were used as waste dumps. In the last ten years or so, however, all of the states on the Atlantic Seaboard have legislated protective wetland laws. The destruction has been greatly reduced, but the toll was

PROFILE OF A TYPICAL COASTAL ZONE ECOSYSTEM
(Barrier Island or Barrier Beach)

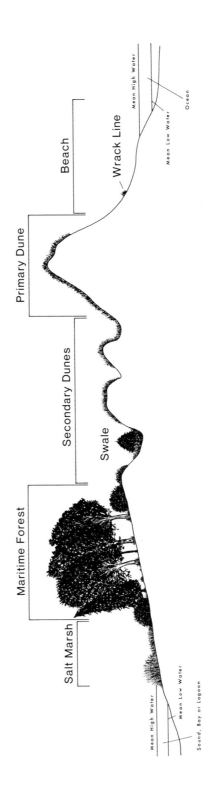

devastating during the years before the laws were enacted. Virginia, for example, was loosing up to 400 acres of tidal wetlands a year until the Wetlands Act was passed in 1972. Since then, fewer than 20 acres per year have been lost.

Federal, state, and private organizations have also been involved in artificial marsh creation. Though most of these projects have been successful, they will likely never replace all the wetlands that man has destroyed over the years, but it is a hopeful endeavor.

Brackish marshes are tidal marshes that grow in waters where the salinity is less than sea strength. They exist along the margins of estuaries and their tributaries. Estuaries are bodies of water, lying at various distances from the ocean, where there is a mixing of both fresh and saline water. Two large estuaries are located near the middle of the Mid-Atlantic Bight, namely Delaware Bay and Chesapeake Bay. Chesapeake Bay is the largest estuary in the United States. It stretches from the mouth of the Susquehanna River to the Virginia capes, a distance of nearly 200 miles, and it varies in width from 5 to 30 miles. Brackish marshes can be found along the shores of estuaries as fringes, perhaps a continuous green band stretching unbroken for a mile or more, in coves, behind spits, in tidal rivers or creeks, or in embayments. They are largely grass dominated, but various species of sedges, rushes, and broadleaf species are also common. Diversity of plant speciation increases with reduced salinity.

Although Saltmarsh Cordgrass still dominates in the intertidal zone (between mean low tide and mean high tide), other species that can tolerate low or moderately saline waters are found here — species such as Big Cordgrass, a giant that may grow to 15 feet tall, Chairmaker's Rush, which for years was used for caning chairs, and Saltmarsh Bulrush, whose seeds are relished by waterfowl.

Perhaps the least understood types of wetlands along the coast are the tidal freshwater marshes and swamps. Basically, the major difference between a marsh and a swamp is that marshes are dominated by herbaceous (non-woody) vegetation, and swamps are dominated by trees. These tidal wetlands usually trace the margins of major tidal rivers, which may be found inland from 30 or more than 150 miles from the ocean. In these tidal rivers or large bays, such as Chesapeake Bay and its tributaries, the wedge of saline water is overcome at some point by fresh water coming down from the interior. Here it forms a wedge with the denser saline water concentrated on the bottom and the fresh water riding on top. Where the wedge is located is highly variable. The salinity wedge/freshwater interface migrates up and down with the seasons. It depends upon the distance from the sea and the volume of fresh water drainage. Its movement is also dictated by catastrophic events such as hurricanes, torrential rains, and prolonged droughts. Drought results in the movement of saline water further up rivers or bays, whereas extreme precipitation has the opposite effect. This area of transition may be only a mile or two long or five miles or more. The gradual rise in sea level, as most of the Atlantic Coast is experiencing, is of course having a long-term effect on its movement.

Saline water, as it moves from the ocean through an estuarine system such as Chesapeake Bay and its tributaries, becomes diluted with each increasing mile. This tidally influenced water typically continues many miles above the transition zone (the salt wedge) to the fall line, where the tide is finally overcome by fresh water drainage from the uplands. The fall line, where tidal action is dissipated, is the boundary between the piedmont and the coastal plain. The piedmont is a physiographic region, usually hilly, lying between the Appalachian mountains and the coastal plain. In many cases the changes in topography are obvious and abrupt. Rapids and rocky bottoms replace the fine sediments characteristic of tidal rivers. Tidal freshwater wetlands are often found between the limits of the salinity wedge and the fall line. The wetlands have developed from sediments deposited by meandering rivers. From the air they may appear as a series of invaginations or peninsulas separated only by the river channel.

A striking difference between freshwater marshes and saline marshes, both of which are prolific, is the diversity of the vegetation. Salt marshes support only a few species (they are very often 90 percent Saltmarsh Cordgrass) because salinity is a very limiting factor. Investigators have found as many as fifty different species of vascular plants in certain freshwater marshes. At the peak of the growing season native species wax luxuriant, causing the marshes to appear subtropical and exotic. Plants lending to this aspect are Arrow Arum with its large, fleshy, triangular leaves, Pickerelweed with its succulent, heart-shaped leaves and spike of bright blue flowers, Lotus Lily with its massive, round, floating leaves and huge pale yellow blooms, and Marsh Hibiscus with its striking white flowers with red centers. Of all the coastal plant communities, these freshwater marshes are the most colorful, especially during midsummer to late summer.

Tidal swamps, dominated by such trees as Bald Cypress, Black Gum, Tupelo Gum, and Red Maple, are often closely associated with freshwater marshes. There is often ecological evidence of an ecotone or transition zone between the two wetland types. Swamps have many of the same herbaceous plants as the marshes, but the diversity within the swamp is not as great, mostly because of shading. Certain species of shrubs, however, are more common in swamps than in marshes.

In this region, some of the most extensive freshwater tidal wetlands are found in the tributary rivers of the Chesapeake Bay and those that empty into Albermarle and Pamlico sounds in North Carolina. These rivers are productive spawning and nursery areas for anadromous fishes such as shad, herring, and striped bass.

For the reader's convenience this field guide is organized into three parts based primarily on ecological habitats: (1) plants of the beach, dunes, and maritime forest, (2) plants of salt and brackish marshes, and (3) plants of tidal freshwater marshes and swamps. In general, the individual species within each part are presented as they would typically appear proceeding from the water/shore interface toward the uplands or inland. In part 1, for example, the sequence is: the beach/ primary dune, secondary dune, shrub zone, maritime forest. In part 2 the order is: the intertidal zone (Saltmarsh Cordgrass), meadow/rush community, saltbush community. The freshwater tidal wetland species (part 3) are presented as follows: the intertidal zone (Arrow Arum/ Pickerelweed), high marsh (diverse community), shrub/swamp. An introduction to each part briefly describes the habitats and plant communities and is followed by individual treatments of the plants. Plant species are illustrated on the left and described on the right. Each drawing appears with an approximate scale. The descriptions include diagnostic characteristics, distribution, ecological relationships, and other information. The guide is thoroughly indexed and a key is provided for use in the field. All plants are described and illustrated in flower or fruit or both. Immature plants are more difficult to identify and their identification goes beyond the scope of this book. While using this guide, please remember that there are often restrictions on collecting plants in federal, state, and local parks and refuges.

A Key to Common Plants of the Mid-Atlantic Coast

(as found in text)

A. Grasses or Grass-like Plants:
Grasses, Sedges, Rushes, Cattails, Sweet Flag

B. Plants with Conspicuous*
Flowers or Pod-like Inflorescences

*Easily observed without a hand lens

C.   Woody Plants:
Trees and Shrubs

D.   Plants without Leaves and Plants without Flowers

Part One

Plants of the Beach, Dunes, and Maritime Forest

MOST OF THE OCEAN FRONT of the Mid-Atlantic Coast is low and sandy, unlike the coast of New England with its rugged cliffs, rocks, and cobble—with exceptions such as Cape Cod. From Long Island south, most of the interface between land and sea along the Mid-Atlantic Coast is a series of barrier beaches or barrier islands.

A barrier beach is a long, narrow, sandy strip that runs parallel to the mainland but at some point is also connected to it. Typically there is a series of shallow bays or sounds between a barrier beach and the mainland. Barrier islands are much the same except that they are islands, typically occurring in a series, separated from one another only by narrow inlets. Both barriers are seldom more than a mile wide, and more often than not they provide but a few hundred yards' buffer between sea and sound.

Beach, dune, and maritime forest species are found on these tenuous barriers, often as components of well-defined communities. Many of these same plants are also found along the shores of major estuaries (such as Chesapeake Bay and its tributaries) where sand is the major substrate.

The following communities are distinctive throughout the Mid-Atlantic Bight.

The Beach Community

A sparse plant community occurs in a narrow, often discontinuous band at the upper zone of the beach, near the seaward base or toe of the primary dune. This area is known as the wrack line. Here storm-lashed surf and spring tides deposit flotsam of various description including fragments of vegetation such as eelgrass, marsh grass, and seaweeds (algae). This detritus, along with driftwood, bottles, cans, and other debris, modifies an otherwise barren, nearly sterile, and windswept backshore. Here, despite incredible odds, grow a few species of unique and very hardy plants. Decaying plant fragments eventually provide organic nutrients necessary for plant growth, and wrack line flotsam acts as a barrier to windblown sand, protecting germinating seeds and young sprigs. However, salt spray, reflected heat, and severe storms are only some of the adverse conditions these pioneer species must tolerate.

The plants that live in this zone have adaptive mechanisms that aid in their survival. In addition to succulence, a characteristic of Sea Rocket, some species have small leaves (1/4 to 1/2 of an inch long and 1/16 to 1/8 of an inch wide) that help reduce water loss. All plants transpire, that is, water vapor is lost through microscopic openings, stomata, found mainly on the leaf surfaces. Plants with very small leaves are more efficient in conserving water than plants with large leaves. Their comparatively smaller surface area has fewer stomata, resulting in less water lost. Certain beach and dune species have dense, minute hairs, not only on the leaves but over most of the plant, that help insulate the plant from heat. In some species the hairs are light gray or white and to some extent reflect sunlight. The leaves of still other species have a waxy coating (cuticle) that reduces dessication and offers protection from salt spray. In some plants the adaptive mechanisms are not as obvious; their internal physiology and metabolism may compensate for the rigors of the harsh environment.

The Primary Dune Community

The dunes that face the sea, the primary dunes, if vegetated at all, are dominated by grass communities, chiefly by American Beach Grass, which ranges from New England south to North Carolina. Another primary dune grass, Sea Oats, ranges from southeast Virginia to the Gulf Coast. American Beach Grass grows naturally so successfully on primary dunes that it is widely planted in dune stabilization projects. It has been extensively planted on the Outer Banks, an area beyond its natural range.

Both Sea Oats and American Beach Grass have the ability to withstand salt spray, high wind velocities, intense reflected heat (resulting in increased evaporation), and accreting sand. Very few species are able to withstand all of these factors, especially accreting sand. But these two seem to thrive under such extreme circumstances. Both respond to sand burial by developing a vertical rhizome. After the plant is buried and accretion subsides, an upright rhizome grows to the surface and produces a young sprig or sprigs that eventually mature. This sequence can happen over and over again. Where primary dunes have been cut through by hurricanes, one can observe this interesting survival mechanism. The profile will reveal vestiges of grass clumps at various levels, with their associated vertical and horizontal rhizomes extending as deep as 30 feet below the top of the dune. The roots of these amazing plants are usually embedded near ther upper parts of the water table, up to 40 feet below the apex of the dune.

Strong winds flex the fruiting stems of these plants to the point where they scribe crescent-like troughs in the sand. Seeds from the plants are abraded off the fruiting heads and are deposited in the depressions. If the grooves are deep enough, the seeds will not be blown away. Eventually some seeds germinate and the population enlarges. Animal tracks, such as deer tracks, also serve as depositories for seeds. The primary means of propagation of dune grasses, however, is vegetatively by underground rhizomes.

Other species are found here, such as Running Dune Grass, Beach Pea, and Dune Bean, but these species seldom predominate on primary dunes.

The Secondary Dune (Dune Field) Community

A field of low secondary dunes is typically found behind the primary dunes on established and relatively stable coastal barrier islands. Here the environment is less harsh than on the primary dune. The fore dunes act as barriers to onshore winds and salt spray, reducing their effects on the plant communities behind them. Denser vegetative cover in this zone reduces surface temperatures and evaporation from the substrate.

Shrub communities such as those discussed above are very common along the Atlantic Coast. They are often very dense, making it difficult to walk through. Shrub communities are also excellent habitats for wildlife. The fruits of Bay Berry, Wax Myrtle, and Poison Ivy are eaten by various birds. Beach Plum is a favorite of raccoons who live in the maritime forest. It is also popular among the people who live on or frequent coastal barrier islands. Its fruit, though less than half the size of a domestic plum, is nevertheless sweet and worth searching for in the fall. The plums can be made into a tasty jam as well. However, one must exercise caution while searching and picking because Beach Plum and Poison Ivy often grow together in these shrubby communities.

Along the secondary dune fields of the Atlantic Coast, the most predominant species is another grass, Saltmeadow Hay, which is not only common on these low dunes but which also forms meadows in salt and brackish marshes. Other species that typically grow here are Dusty Miller, Sand Bur, Switch Grass, Pinweed, Bay Berry, Wax Myrtle, and Beach Heather, which forms dense, low, shrubby patches.

Many dune field species have adaptive features that help them to survive. Their leaf surface may be coated with a hard waxy substance known as cuticle, which reduces the effect of excessive transpiration and salt spray. A number of plants are covered by dense hairs that insulate the plant from heat. Dusty Miller and Beach Heather have this characteristic. Other adaptive mechanisms are discussed in the accompanying plant descriptions.

A wetland community usually develops in low depressions among the dunes and in old (inactive) blowout areas where moist sand lies above the water table. Herbaceous wetland species are the first to invade — rushes, sedges, ferns, Marsh Hibiscus, and smartweeds, to name a few. Eventually shrubs will begin to grow — Bay Berry, Wax Myrtle, Poison Ivy, Beach Plum, Groundsel Tree (Silvering), Winged Sumac, and others.

The maritime forest, which lies just behind the secondary dunes, also has a buffering effect on the plant communities of this habitat. The tree canopy, which can be up to 40 to 60 feet tall in a mature maritime forest, can greatly reduce the velocity of offshore winds. The secondary dunes are only fully exposed to southerly or northerly winds as a result. Under the influence of these moderating conditions, dense and diverse vegetational communities develop.

The Maritime Forest

Maritime forests are the most stable of the coastal communities. Typically they develop behind the dune fields, usually in low areas adjacent to the marshes on the sound side. The predominant species in the northern part of the Mid-Atlantic region (Long Island and New Jersey) are Pitch Pine, Wild Black Cherry, American Holly, Sassafras, Post Oak, and Red Cedar. The Sunken Forest on Fire Island has developed on low dunes that slope towards Great South Bay. American Holly is common here and on Sandy Hook, New Jersey. Black Gum is often the dominant tree in low depressions in these forests.

Farther south, Loblolly Pine replaces Pitch Pine, and Live Oak outcompetes Post Oak. Other species remain the same throughout the region except for Persimmon and Toothache Tree, which are occasionally found in southern coastal woodlands. An unusual shrubby plant grows under the canopy of Loblolly Pine in the coastal woodlands from Cape Hatteras south to the Gulf. Dwarf Palmetto with its fan-like leaves often forms rather dense thickets that are nearly impenetrable.

Characteristically, the canopies of these hardy maritime forests are sculptured by strong winds and salt spray. The toxic effect of salt often kills the tender terminal buds, but the more protected lateral buds develop, resulting in dense, wedge-shaped canopies. This is particularly true where the maritime forest is close to the ocean.

Maritime forests are not found on all coastal barriers, especially if the beach and the dunes are in a dynamic state of flux. In a number of cases, barrier islands and other coastal formations are advancing towards the mainland at a rate of 30 feet or more per year. On islands where there is no vegetation to bind the sand, mobile dunes have buried everything in their paths, including vehicles, beach houses, and whole forests. Some dwellings have been buried for 60 years or more only to be exposed again as relics of the past. Marsh peat, 50 years ago a part of the salt marsh behind the dunes, now lies beyond the surf zone under water. Some beaches at low tide reveal the ancient stumps of a maritime forest.

x ½

American Beach Grass
Beach Grass
Ammophila breviligulata Fern.

From New England to North Carolina, American Beach Grass is the most common plant that grows on primary dunes. Its flowering spike distinguishes it from other dune grasses. The flowers of grasses (called florets) are minute and lack colorful petals and sepals. Beach Grass flowers are compacted into a cylindrical spike, which in late summer turns from green to light gray as the seeds form. Its culms (stems) stand from 2 to 4 feet high. The flowering spike is surrounded by a tuft of long, narrow, and pointed leaves.

Beach Grass has excellent sand-binding abilities and can tolerate and even thrive to some degree on being buried by shifting sand. Only one other beach plant can withstand such conditions, and that is Sea Oats, which has a more southern range. When the individual culms of these two grasses are buried by sand, the plants respond by sending up a vertical rhizome. At the tip of the rhizome a new plant is produced. This process takes place after each successive burial. On very high dunes the distance from the plant on the top of the dune to the tip of the main root below may be 40 feet or more. In between, there may be remnants of plants that have been buried over the years. Despite this incredible adaptive feature, both Beach Grass and Sea Oats are susceptible to compaction and the wear and tear of foot and vehicular traffic. Seedlings of Beach Grass and Sea Oats are often planted in dune restoration projects.

x ½

Sea Oats
Uniola paniculata L.

This tall, stately grass is one of the most important primary dune plants along the southern Atlantic Coast. It stands 3 to 6 feet tall and its long narrow leaves are usually less than 1/2 of an inch wide. Its robust seed head (a panicle of numerous wafer-like spikelets) is easily distinguished from American Beach Grass with its rather narrow, dense, flowering spike. In late summer or early fall the Sea Oats seed head turns a bronze-yellow color, whereas the spike of Beach Grass matures to a dull gray. Sea Oats produces few viable seeds, and propagates chiefly by rhizomes.

Both Sea Oats and American Beach Grass are highly adaptive to wind, accreting sand, salt spray, and dry conditions. Because of their sand-binding capabilities, which help to stabilize primary dunes, they are important natural resources in a dune field and should not be disturbed. See the text under American Beach Grass and the preface to this part for more information on their propagation and sand-binding characteristics.

Sea Oats ranges along the Atlantic Seaboard south from Virginia to the Gulf Coast. It is nearly always found on primary dunes, seldom on secondary dunes.

x ½

Seaside Goldenrod
Solidago sempervirens L.

During late summer or early fall, one of the most striking plants in the coastal zone is Seaside Goldenrod. This tall, leafy perennial produces a spray of bright yellow blooms typical of Goldenrods. Its leaves are dark green and fleshy and are produced in profusion along the entire length of the stem, which may be as much as 6 feet tall. It is typically found on the backsides of primary dunes, on low secondary dunes, or along the edge of salt marshes.

Seaside Goldenrod is found in saline environments along the Atlantic Coast and the Gulf of Mexico.

x ½

Dusty Miller
Artemisia stelleriana Besser

Dusty Miller is an introduced plant found mainly on secondary dunes. Commonly used as an ornamental border plant in flower gardens because of its unusual and attractive foliage, over the years it has escaped from these domestic habitats and has adapted well to dry sandy dunes from Quebec to Virginia. Originally, Dusty Miller came from Asia and Japan where it grows wild.

Its lobed silvery-gray leaves have dense whitish hairs on both sides, giving the foliage a velvety appearance. As are many dune species, Dusty Miller is a perennial and spreads by creeping underground stems called rhizomes. Although the foliage is mostly low or creeping in posture, at the peak of the growing season the plant produces a flowering stem (pictured) that may be over 2 feet tall. This reproductive stem may have a large number of flower heads. Each head bears many tiny, almost inconspicuous yellow flowers, a characteristic of the Compositae or Aster family to which this plant belongs.

X ¾

Short Dune Grass
Running Beach Grass
Panicum amarum Ell.

Short Dune Grass, which stands 1 to 2 feet tall, is found on dunes from the New England area to the Gulf Coast. Compared to American Beach Grass and Sea Oats, which are light green in color, the leaves of Short Dune Grass are a distinguishing light blue-green. The seed head, visible from midsummer to autumn, is a sparse, narrow panicle bearing small, ellipsoid seeds. Unlike Beach Grass and Sea Oats, Short Dune Grass is not as highly adapted to accreting sand. The specialized growth systems of Beach Grass and Sea Oats can keep up with sand build-up, but Short Dune Grass will eventually become buried by large amounts of shifting sands and will die. Its sand-binding abilities are hence limited. Where there are optimal growing conditions (reduced sand accretion and salt spray), this grass often forms dense mats of vegetation originating from its underground rhizomes. Short Dune Grass is found on the top and landward side of primary dunes and on secondary dunes.

X ³⁄₄

Sea Rocket

Cakile edentula (Bigelow) Hooker

Sea Rocket usually occupies the zone between the toe of a primary dune and the wrack line on the beach. *Cakile* is a somewhat prostrate, low-growing green plant that turns yellow in the fall. Its succulent, fleshy stems and leaves store water, helping to maintain an optimal water balance within the plant in its saline environment, which it tolerates quite well. Its small flowers are lavender or light blue, occasionally white. Thick, fleshy green fruits (pictured) develop late in the growing season. Although Sea Rocket does not have the sand-binding qualities of the beach grasses, it is native to this dynamic zone between the toe of the primary dune and the mean high water line. It is often found with Russian Thistle and Cocklebur, especially if there is a protective wrack line.

This halophic plant ranges from the Canadian Maritime Provinces to Florida.

x 1

Seaside Spurge
Euphorbia polygonifolia L.

Seaside Spurge is a low-growing small-leaved plant typical of the beach and dune environment. Plants such as Seaside Spurge, Russian Thistle, Seabeach Sandwort, and Beach Heather have diminutive foliage and white flowers. (The flowers of Seaside Spurge do not last long, so one seldom sees the plant in bloom.) Its reduced characteristic form (habit) helps the plant to survive the dry, windy, salt spray environment. The smaller leaves have fewer stomata (microscopic openings that regulate water loss or transpiration) through which to lose water. The more water retained, the greater the survival rate. That is, larger, broad-leaved species are less apt to survive in this particular environment.

Along its decumbent (runner-like) stems, Seaside Spurge produces roots that attach the plant closely to the sand surface, thereby reducing wind abrasion. When this plant is crushed or broken, a milky, sticky sap exudes. A large portion of this substance is latex, characteristic of most euphorbs. Latex may aid in water retention.

Seaside Spurge is found along most of the Atlantic Coast from Quebec to Georgia. Its habitat is variable, occurring just above the wrack line, behind primary dunes or on secondary dunes. It propagates by both roots and seeds. The fruiting stage is illustrated.

x 1

Russian Thistle
Common Saltwort
Salsola kali L.

The spiny annual called Russian Thistle, an introduced plant from
Eurasia, is often considered a troublesome weed in semiarid areas in
the western states, but it is quite restricted to coastal dunes and the
wrack line of upper beaches on the Eastern Seaboard. *Salsola*, which
stands from 1 to 3 feet tall, is not a true thistle, but its fleshy, long,
narrow leaves do culminate in sharp spiny tips. Late in the growing
season the plants often turn a red or pink color. They propagate by
seeds. In the drawing the shorter clusters are the flowers. It is difficult
to see them clearly without a hand lens. In winter, dead plants are
often blown loose and collectively form tumbleweeds. The plant is
often associated with Sea Rocket in the upper beach zone above the
reach of daily high tides. It ranges from Labrador to the Gulf Coast.

x ¼

Cocklebur
Xanthium strumarium L.

The Cocklebur plant is often found at the base of the primary dune,
at the upper beach level, or in sand overwash areas. It grows in
association with (though is less successful and plentiful than) Sea
Rocket, Russian Thistle, and Seaside Spurge. It has large, 2- to 4-inch-
wide, somewhat heart-shaped leaves, rough stems that may have
several branches, and characteristic spiny cocklebur seeds that develop
late in the growing season. Its small rather nondescript flowers are
difficult to describe. Cocklebur seeds are commonly transported by
animals and people as the spiny seeds attach readily to fur and
clothing. Cocklebur is not strictly a coastal species but is found as a
weed in fields, pastures, and along roadsides throughout large
portions of North America.

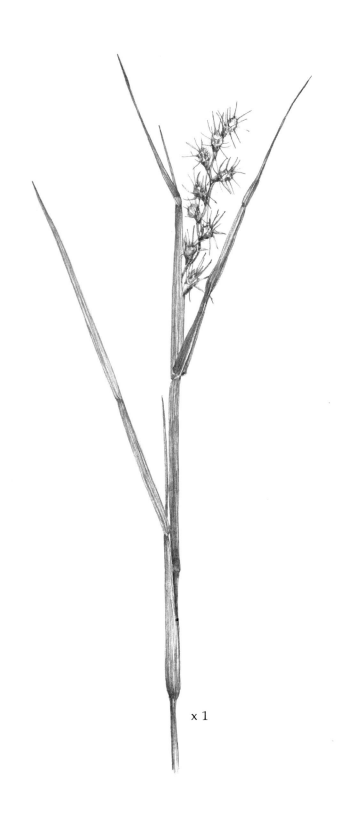

x 1

Sand Bur
Sandspurs
Cenchrus tribuloides L.

At one time or another, surely every man, woman, child, and pet has stepped on the spiny seeds of Sand Bur while at the beach. There are several different species of this grass, and all have a particularly bad reputation — rightly so because their spiny seeds have minute barb-like bristles, that are quite painful when lodged in the skin.

Sand Bur has relatively short leaf blades and obvious, flattened leaf sheaths. It is largely confined to coastal dunes from New York to the Gulf Coast, where generally it is found on secondary dunes and on the backsides of primary dunes. Other species can be found inland in dry sandy pastures, in open pine woods, or on barrens. Sand Bur may grow as one or two culms or in sparse tufts. Typically it stands from 1 to 1-1/2 feet high. After flowering, it produces seeds in late June and July; the seeds are green at first, then turn tan. By August the plant weakens, lies flat on the ground, and often becomes rooted there. It is, however, an annual and reproduces by seed only. The plant is illustrated in seed.

Despite its formidable seeds, Sand Bur does have redeeming qualities as a sand binder. When the stems or culms lie flat in late summer, the leaf nodes often produce roots where they touch the sand, thereby securing the lax culms. The low profile and the rooted stems are adaptive features that reduce wind abrasion and increase water uptake.

X ¾

Switch Grass
Panicum virgatum L.

Switch Grass is commonly found growing on low dunes and in tufts along the upper, drier margins of salt and brackish marshes. It is seldom found on active dunes because it cannot tolerate burial as well as American Beach Grass or Sea Oats. The open, delicately branched panicle with tiny florets at the tips of its branches is the distinguishing feature of *Panicum.* As with most grasses, the flowers are inconspicuous and not colorful. Its long, narrow leaves are concentrated in basal clumps or tufts. Leaves of the previous season are usually present, matted radially around the tuft. The plant propagates by seeds and vegetatively via rhizomes.

Switch Grass is often associated with Groundsel Tree and Saltmarsh Foxtail Grass in drier parts of the marsh. It appears to invade higher parts that have been burned, often replacing marsh meadows.

Switch Grass is common along the Atlantic and Gulf coasts but is also found interior as far west and north as Montana. It is pictured here in seed.

x 1

Dune Bean
Beach Bean
Strophyostyles helvola (L.) Ell.

Dune Bean, an annual, is a trailing and twining vine that occupies various habitats in the dune/beach system. It has a characteristic bean or legume flower that is rose or purplish when mature. It also produces a typical bean pod with seeds. Flowers and pods occur together on the same vine throughout the summer. The leaves are divided into three separate leaflets. The combination of these three features — flower, pod, and leaf — will distinguish this vine from many other plants that live in the same habitat. Dune Bean is seldom found beyond the secondary dunes or on the beach (wrack line). It apparently cannot tolerate salt spray and flooding like other wrack line or primary dune species.

When the seeds of this plant are released from the pods they are likely eaten by birds and other rodents that live in the maritime forest or shrub community.

Dune Bean ranges throughout most of the eastern United States and the Great Lakes region as well as throughout the Atlantic coastal region. Despite its name, it is not strictly a dune species but can be found in maritime forests and in interior, open woodland habitats.

X ¾

Prickly Pear Cactus
Opuntia compressa (Salisb.) Macbr.

It is fitting that one find a cactus growing on coastal dunes. Not to the contrary, Prickly Pear Cactus is frequently found along the Mid-Atlantic Coast. This cactus often forms large, spreading mats, which in summer produce big pale yellow blooms with red centers. In the fall, the reddish-purple fruits are edible and can be made into cactus jam. The fruits should be peeled however, to rid them of minute bristles. This particular cactus has few or no spines, but its many tiny bristles (glochids) irritate the skin if the plant is handled.

Opuntia compressa is found on secondary dunes throughout the Mid-Atlantic Coast as well as in dry areas in the interior.

× 3/4

Pinweed
Lechea maritima Leggett

Pinweed is typical of the low, small-leaved, scrubby perennials that survive in the adverse coastal environment. It ranges in height from 6 inches to 1-1/2 feet. Its tiny leaves are densely crowded on basal branches that may be partially buried by wind-blown sand. The leaves are gray-green in appearance because of minute, appressed hairs. These nearly microscopic hairs retard the loss of moisture through the leaves and serve as an insulating mechanism against solar radiation. Adaptive characteristics such as these are not unusual among dune vegetation. At the peak of the growing season the plant produces an upright head (panicle) of tiny red flowers, as pictured.

Pinweed is found behind primary dunes and on secondary dunes. This species is rare in coastal areas from New England south to Virginia. A similar species, *Lechea leggettii*, is more common along the Atlantic and Gulf coasts. The leaves of this plant are not as hairy as the former.

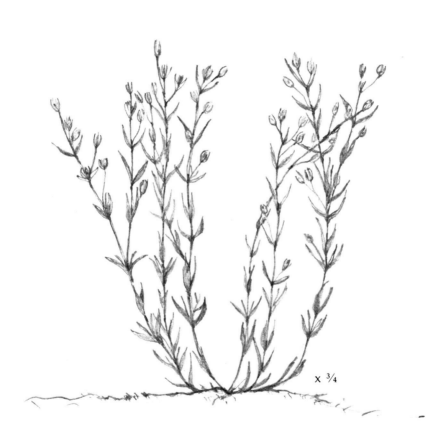

X ¾

Seabeach Sandwort

Arenaria lanuginosa (Michaux) Rohrback

This small plant, 3 to 5 inches tall, is usually found on the margin of swales between or behind the primary dunes. Sandwort appears too delicate for the rigorous coastal environment, and in fact the plants appear more vigorous where somewhat protected from salt spray, excessive sand accretion, and wind. The leaves are small and narrow and the white flowers are not conspicuous.

Seabeach Sandwort is a southern plant that ranges from southeastern Virginia to tropical America.

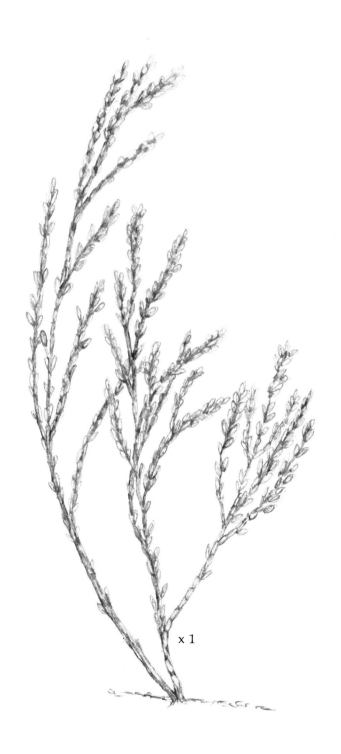

x 1

Beach Heather
Hudsonia tomentosa Nuttall

Beach Heather is a low, spreading, shrubby plant that rarely grows over a foot tall. The leaves are scale-like, resembling those of a cedar tree, and are densely covered with short, whitish hairs that give these little shrubs a "mildewy" appearance. At the peak of the growing season, tiny yellow flowers bloom.

Beach Heather generally grows on the edges of blowout areas in the dunes. During periods of drought the plants appear gray and lifeless. Several days after a heavy rain, however, they are able to generate new growth. *Hudsonia tomentosa* is more common in the New England area than the Mid-Atlantic area, but it ranges as far south as North Carolina, where it is found infrequently.

X ¾

Three-awn Grass
Poverty Grass
Aristida tuberculosa Nuttall

Three-awn Grass, sometimes called Poverty Grass because it grows well on poor soil, is usually found growing on dry sand in coastal dune fields and on pine barrens. It is a short (1 to 2-1/2 feet tall), wiry grass with three long, twisted, stiff appendages or awns that originate from the base of each floret. The awns are twisted into a column to about midway their entire length. At this point the column divides into the three separate awns, which twist outward into an almost horizontal position, hence the name Three-awn Grass. In the drawing the leaves are at the base of the plant; they are longer and broader than the awns, and they are not twisted. The fruiting (seed) stage is illustrated. Three-awn Grass is an annual and propagates by seeds only.

Three-awn Grass is sometimes locally abundant on stabilized (no longer active) blowout areas, but it is not as common as other dune grasses throughout its range from New England to Georgia.

x ¹/₂

Mexican Tea
Chenopodium ambrosiodes L.

Mexican Tea is a 3- to 6-foot-tall herb of rank growth and dubious aromatic qualities. It stinks! The specific epithet *ambrosiodes* is definitely a misnomer. Though a native of South America, Mexican Tea has established itself in various habitats throughout the United States. Like most weedy species, it likes to invade disturbed areas, such as overwash flats. Weedy plants are good invaders primarily because their natural enemies — insects, fungi, and bacteria — are not established in the new area; therefore, introduced plants flourish in the absence of biological controls.

Grooves run the length of the stem of this plant, and its foliage is somewhat sticky because of minute glands that secrete sap. The flowers are green without showy petals.

Mexican Tea is sometimes associated with Cocklebur, another weedy plant. It resembles Lamb's-quarters, a closely related plant whose leaves can be eaten as greens. Mexican Tea is more common along southern shores than it is in the north.

X $^1/_{16}$

Adam's Needle
Yucca
Bear Grass
Yucca filamentosa L.

Colonies of Yucca lend a desert-like aspect to coastal dunes. The plant is characterized by a dense rosette of leathery, evergreen, linear, sharp-pointed leaves. At the peak of the growing season, June through August, each plant produces a spreading panicle of white or cream-colored, bell-shaped flowers. This particular species, *Yucca filamentosa,* has fraying whitish threads along its leaf margins. The leaves are grayish-green. Though native to the coastal area from Maryland to Georgia, it is often planted as an ornamental and can be found throughout the South. *Yucca* is well adapted to dry, sandy, infertile environments. It is found behind primary dunes, on low dunes, and on the edges of maritime forests.

X ³/₄

Croton

Croton punctatus Jacquin

Croton is a leafy, herbaceous plant found on coastal dunes and beaches from North Carolina to the Gulf Coast. In North Carolina it is associated with Sea Rocket and Seaside Spurge along the upper beach areas above the high tide zone. It is often found associated with Sea Oats on the primary dune and with Saltmeadow Hay in grassy low dunes.

Croton gives a mealy or velvety appearance because of dense, minute, stellate hairs (visible only with a hand lens) that cover the entire plant, including fruits and flowers.

The flowers of this plant, which are globular and not very distinguishing, consist mainly of reproductive organs (stamens and pistils). They do not have petals; the sepals are green and mealy like the rest of the plant. The fruits remain in the cup-like calyx (made of fused sepals) until the plant decays in winter. The seed coat is gray. The obvious floral characteristics are essentially the same whether it is in flower or in fruit. Croton propagates by seeds, which are eaten by birds and perhaps mice from the maritime forest and shrub communities.

As with most plants, this herb is most easily identified in mid-summer.

x ⅓

Beach Pea

Lathyrus maritimus (L.) Bigel.

Beach Pea is a vine-like perennial often found on low grassy dunes with Saltmeadow Hay. Occasionally it is associated with American Beach Grass and Running Dune Grass on primary dunes. The leaves are pinnately compound with fleshy leaflets and a terminal tendril. The tendrils are usually wound around adjacent grasses. The flowers vary in color from purple to magenta and are produced throughout the growing season from June to September. Dark brown seed pods (legumes) are produced throughout much of the growing season. Birds and rodents (mice) eat the peas. Although a number of seeds are produced by each plant, the primary means of Beach Pea propagation is via the underground rhizome. Beach Pea is primarily a plant of the North Atlantic Coast, but disjunct populations are found as far west as the Great Lakes. Beach Pea ranges no farther south than the New Jersey coast.

x ⅛

Dwarf Palmetto
Sabal minor (Jacquin) Persoon

Dwarf Palmetto is a southern coastal shrub that reaches its northern limit in Dare County, North Carolina. *Sabal minor* is frequently found in dense stands in maritime forests dominated by Loblolly Pine and Live Oak and in open low dune areas. Farther south this plant is commonly found with Cabbage Palmetto (*Sabal palmetto*) in coastal habitats, particularly in maritime forests.

The large (up to 3 feet wide), fan-shaped, palmately-divided leaf is distinctive; the plant cannot be confused with any other in this habitat. It stands up to 6 feet tall. At the peak of the growing season, each Palmetto plant produces a large panicle of small, lily-like flowers, a characteristic common to all members of the Palm family (Arecaceae). Late in the season, the inflorescence is transformed into a cluster of berry-like fruits prized by birds.

The leaves and flower stalk (peduncle) originate from underground rhizomes and do not have discernable stems. In the areas where Dwarf Palmetto grows, the subsurface of the soil is laced with rhizomes that produce many flower stalks and leaves. It is difficult to say what constitutes an individual plant—the plant includes a rhizome that may be many feet long and that can produce two or twenty leaves and several flowering stalks. The illustration shows a typical leaf and fruiting stalk.

x 1

Seaside Primrose
Oenothera humifusa Nuttall

This low-growing, yellow-flowered herb can be found on stable primary dunes or on secondary dunes from New Jersey to the Gulf Coast. Pale yellow flowers are produced spring through frost. Elongated, cylindrical fruits may be found among the flowers (as shown) from summer through autumn. The foliage and stems appear pale green as they are densely hairy, a trait that has insulative value. The stems may have several branches. Unfortunately, the leaf shape is highly variable from plant to plant and even on the same plant; the leaf margins may be toothed or not, and the width of the leaves varies.

The 4- to 12-inch-tall plant is perennial and often becomes somewhat woody with age. The woody portion is likely to be covered by drifting sand with only the herbaceous, leafy, flowering portion exposed. Seaside Primrose may be associated with Seaside Spurge, Seaside Goldenrod, Beach Heather, and Prickly Pear Cactus.

x ½

Beach Plum
Prunus maritima Marsh

Beach Plum is a northern coastal shrub that often forms 3- to 7-foot tall thickets dense with several species of shrubs in depressions or swales between low dunes. It can also be found in maritime forests, especially where the canopy is open. From Maine to New Jersey, Beach Plum is usually the major component of these thickets. Other woody species significant in these habitats are Bay Berry, Winged Sumac, Shadbushes or Juneberries, Groundsel Tree or Silvering, and last but not least, Poison Ivy.

The leaves of Beach Plum are alternate on the stem and are finely serrated. This shrub flowers in May; the blossoms are white. The fruiting stage is illustrated.

The fruit of the Beach Plum (purplish-black but occasionally brick red or dull yellow) is prized by those who gather wild foods. It can be eaten fresh or made into sauce, preserves, or pies. Beach Plum thickets provide excellent cover for many wildlife creatures, and the fruits are eaten by a wide range of bird species and a few mammals. Juneberries are edible as well and can be eaten fresh or cooked in the same ways as Beach Plum.

One word of caution, however, for those who gather these delights: be careful of Poison Ivy with its telling white berries and trifoliate leaves.

X ³/₄

Yaupon
Ilex vomitoria Aiton

Yaupon is a small-leaved holly found in dense thickets or at the
margins of maritime forests from southeastern Virginia along the
Atlantic and Gulf coasts and up the Mississippi Valley to Arkansas.
The ellipse-shaped leaves are evergreen, with somewhat wavy
margins, and are alternately arranged on the stem. They are shiny on
top and dull beneath. The flowers have petals and sepals but are
inconspicuous. The berry-like fruit is usually red but can also be
orange or yellow. According to historical accounts, the leaves contain
caffeine and were brewed as hot "black drink" by coastal Indians.
During the late eighteenth century and into the early twentieth
century, the leaves were dried and processed on the Outer Banks of
North Carolina and were sold commercially as Yaupon Tea.

A number of bird species eat the colorful fruit from this shrub.
Yaupon is often associated with American Holly (*Ilex opaca*) on the
coast, but unlike its close relative, it never attains tree-like characteristics or proportions. It stands 5 to 15 feet tall.

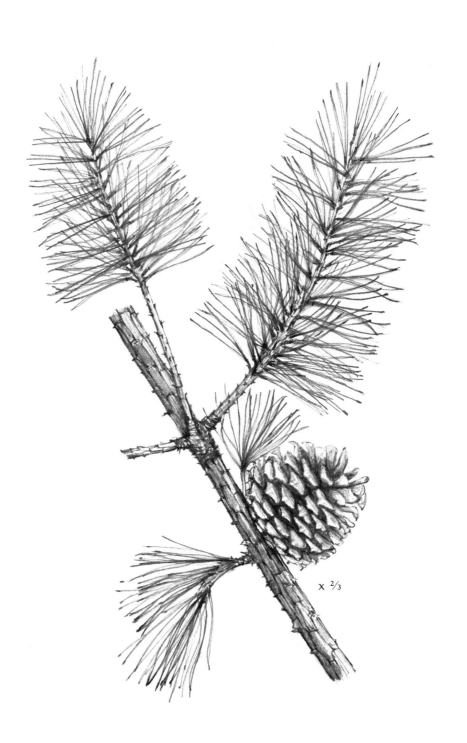

x ⅔

Pitch Pine
Pinus rigida Mill.

Pitch Pine is the predominant conifer of maritime forests in the northern part of the Mid-Atlantic region. Typically it is a component of coastal woodlands and rocky barrens from the Maritime Provinces to the New Jersey coastal plain pine barrens. The distribution of Pitch Pine continues down the Appalachian Mountains and piedmont to Georgia, many miles from the coast. Loblolly Pine, a southern species, is typically found in maritime forests from southern New Jersey to Florida.

Pitch Pine has needles in clusters or fascicles of three in nearly uniform length but varying from 2 to 4 inches long. The cone is globular in shape. Loblolly Pine has longer needles (5 to 10 inches) and a more elongated cone.

Pitch Pine can grow as tall as 50 feet, but is usually 15 to 30 feet high along the coast. In this environment Pitch Pine often has a contorted and windswept canopy, a result of salt spray and wind-blown sand. Years ago the pitch from this tree was processed into a tar used for caulking wooden ships.

Along the coast, Pitch Pines are used as heronries and rookeries, and the dead trees often harbor osprey nests.

x ½

Loblolly Pine
Pinus taeda L.

Loblolly Pine is one of the most common pines of the coastal plains
and piedmont of the Mid–Southern Atlantic states. It is also a major
species of the maritime forest in this same area. Loblolly Pine is a
pioneer or invader tree of old dune fields and is therefore one of the
first trees in the embryonic maritime forest. This is the forest's early
ecological successional phase. Trees such as Loblolly Pine invade
secondary dune fields when the primary dunes are tall enough and
become stable enough through vegetational cover to reduce salt spray
and buffer onshore winds.

Loblolly Pine needles come in bundles or fasicles of threes, 5 to
10 inches long. The cones are 3 to 6 inches long, elongated, and have
a broad base. The canopy of Loblolly Pine is often sculptured by wind-
blown sand and salt spray. The tree can grow as tall as 90 feet, but
15 to 50 feet is the rule on the coast.

Its counterpart in the more northern maritime forests, such as on
Fire Island (Long Island), is Pitch Pine. Loblolly Pine is often
associated with Wild Black Cherry, Live Oak, Red Bay, Red Cedar,
and Sassafras in the maritime forests of Virginia and North Carolina.
Its range is from southern New Jersey to Florida.

These coastal forests are often used by great blue and black
crowned night herons as rookeries or roosting sites. Birds and squirrels
eat the seeds produced by the cones.

X ³/₄

American Holly
Christmas Holly
Ilex opaca Aiton

This familiar and attractive holly is common throughout the south-eastern states but north of Virginia its habitat is somewhat restricted to the coast. American Holly is frequently a part of the shrub and maritime forest community, standing 5 to 15 feet high, but inland it often becomes a large tree, 50 feet or more tall. The shrub's bright red berries and dark, evergreen, leaves with spiny margins are, of course, distinctive. The berries are eaten by several species of birds and are an important food source in an environment where diversity and abundance are limited. Its flowers are tiny, yellow-green, and short-lived.

American Holly is a significant component of the maritime forests (Sunken Forest) on Fire Island (Long Island) and Sandy Hook, New Jersey.

x 1

Bay Berry
Myrica pensylvanica Loisel.

Bay Berry is a shrub commonly found in the coastal environment from the Maritime Provinces to the Gulf Coast. It is often a dominant component of the shrub thicket communities bordering maritime forests. Bay Berry can also be found in swale areas between secondary dunes where the water table is near the surface. Here it is sometimes found with Beach Plum, Groundsel Tree, Poison Ivy, and other shrubs.

The fragrantly spicy, dark green leaves are deciduous, falling in late autumn. The leaves range in size from 2-1/2 to 4 inches long and 1 to 2-1/2 inches wide. Flowers and fruits develop somewhat below the leafy tips of the stem. The conspicuous, waxy, bluish-gray fruits vary from 1/8 to 1/4 inch in diameter. The illustration shows the shrub in the fruiting stage. The waxy substance from the fruits can be melted down and used for making scented candles. The leaves of Bay Berry are not the leaves used for seasoning. Bay leaf (seasoning) actually comes from Red Bay, a small tree often found in low areas of maritime forests farther south.

From southern New Jersey south to the Gulf Coast, the ranges of Bay Berry and Wax Myrtle merge. In this zone, the two species often hybridize, making identification difficult. Bay Berry, Wax Myrtle, and their hybrids are occasionally used as nesting areas for herons.

Myrica cerifera L.

x ³⁄₄

Wax Myrtle

Myrica cerifera L.
Myrica heterophylla Raf.

Wax Myrtle is a tall evergreen shrub that occupies various coastal habitats: on the border between marshes and uplands, in coastal swamps or pocosins, in shrub thickets behind primary dunes, and along the margins of maritime forests. The leathery, dark green leaves have a spicy aroma as well as do the blue-gray, waxy, berry-like fruits. The drawing shows Wax Myrtle in fruit. Note that the berry-like fruits are found below the leafy stem tips. Wax Myrtle can be easily confused with the Bay Berries, *Myrica pensylvanica* and *Myrica heterophylla*. The latter is apparently a hybrid between *Myrica cerifera* and *Myrica pensylvanica*. The Bay Berries have broader leaves and larger fruits than Wax Myrtle (1/16 to 1/8 of an inch), and Wax Myrtle is evergreen whereas Bay Berry is deciduous.

On Virginia's Eastern Shore, certain Myrtle thickets serve as heronries. On some of the heavily used sites the guano becomes so thick that the shrubs are eventually killed. Tree swallows feed upon the fruits in the fall.

Wax Myrtle ranges along the coast from southern New Jersey to the Gulf of Mexico.

x ½

Sassafras
Sassafras albidum (Nuttall) Nees

Sassafras, ubiquitous throughout much of the eastern and southern United States, is also often encountered in the maritime forest. It usually grows 15 to 30 feet tall here, though it can reach heights of 60 feet elsewhere. Along with Loblolly Pine, Sassafras is often a pioneer tree of a developing maritime forest. As the forest becomes more mature, this tree is often outcompeted by other species such as Live Oak and Wild Black Cherry: Sassafras is a fast-growing tree in open areas. As the trees grow tall and provide shade, the seedlings of Sassafras die out because they are not shade-tolerant. The seedlings of other species, oaks for example, are shade-tolerant. Eventually, after many years of course, even the taller Sassafras trees die out from the shade. Though other factors are involved, the controlling factor is shade.

Sassafras is easily identified by its unusual characteristic of sporting three differently-shaped leaves on the same tree. These shapes are three-lobed, mitten-shaped (right-lobed or left-lobed), and unlobed or simple, ellipse-shaped. The bark, leaves, and roots have an aromatic, spicy odor similar to Red Bay, to which Sassafras is related. In the past, aromatic oil was extracted from the bark and roots and used for flavoring root beer and soaps. The bark of the root continues to be used for the brewing of sassafras tea.

The flowers of Sassafras are greenish-yellow, inconspicuous, and last only a few days.

x ½

Red Bay
Persea borbonia (L.) Sprengel.

Red Bay is an attractive small tree that can grow up to 50 feet tall but seldom grows over 30 in maritime forests. It has shiny, evergreen, lance-like leaves and reddish-brown bark with a faintly spicy fragrance. The tree's aromatic leaves—bay leaves—are used to flavor various foods. Its flowers are yellow-green, small, and short-lived (one or two weeks). The flowers are relatively inconspicuous in the spring, but in autumn dark blue or black plum-like, 1/4- to 3/8-inch-round fruits are obvious. They are eaten by several species of birds. The fruiting stage, September through October, is illustrated.

Red Bay is often found in swamps, streams, and/or pocosins of the coastal plain in general. It is seldom abundant in the maritime forest because the swales (low wet depressions) in these forests are smaller in area than the rest of the forest. The roots of Red Bay can tolerate the low oxygen levels found in the saturated soil of the swales. Although it ranges from southern Delaware to coastal Texas, Red Bay is more common from Virginia south.

X $^3/_4$

Wild Black Cherry
Prunus serotina Ehrhart

Wild Black Cherry, a common tree of deciduous forests in the eastern United States, is also a component of the maritime forest. It often grows in association with Sassafras, Pitch and Loblolly pines, Post Oak, Live Oak, and American Holly in the maritime forests of the Mid-Atlantic region. The maritime Wild Black Cherries, however, do not attain the stately trunk and canopy of the Black Cherries of the interior woodlands, which attain heights of 70 feet. Wind and salt spray affect the growth pattern, typically resulting in a shorter and rather contorted trunk and canopy. Wild Black Cherry seldom grows taller than 50 feet in the harsh maritime environment. One would think it would prefer areas protected by other, more tolerant trees such as Live Oak — but it is found in the more exposed parts of the forest.

The leaves of this tree are simple, alternately arranged, and have serrated margins. The tree produces white flowers in April and May. In the summer, Wild Black Cherry trees are often laden with small black fruits (cherries), much favored by different species of birds in an environment that has a scarcity of such food.

X ¾

Live Oak
Quercus virginiana Miller

Live Oak is an evergreen tree with wide-spreading branches. In many cases the width of the canopy is more than twice the height of the tree. The leaves are thick, dark green, and glossy. A hard, waxy cuticle that covers the leaves helps the tree to withstand sand-laden winds and salt spray.

Live Oak is a major component of the maritime forest from southeastern Virginia to Florida on the Atlantic Coast and from Florida to Texas on the Gulf Coast. In the southern part of the Mid-Atlantic Coast (Virginia and North Carolina), this species is usually associated with Loblolly Pine in well-established maritime forests.

The trees are often sculptured by prevailing onshore winds and salt spray. The characteristic wedge-shaped canopies are a result of the toxic effects of salt, which kills the terminal buds; the more protected lateral buds then form dense, peculiar foliage. Squirrels and deer often eat the acorns.

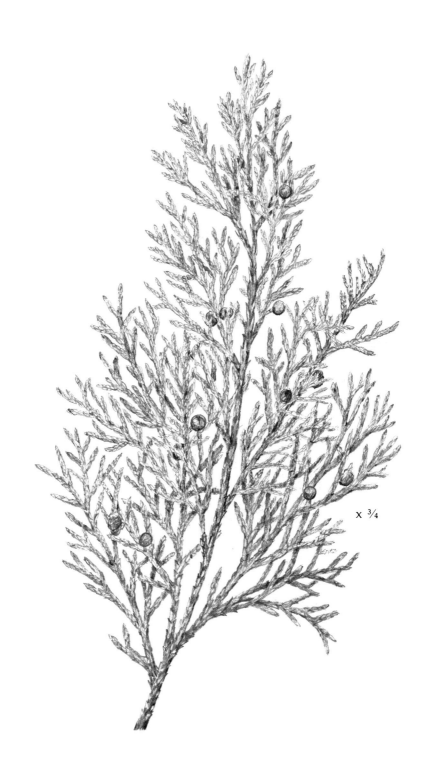

X ¾

Red Cedar
Juniper
Juniperus virginiana L.

Red Cedar or Juniper, the latter the more appropriate common name, is sometimes associated with other trees of the maritime forests in this region. It is found in various locations but seems to prefer more interior areas; it is not as tolerant of salt spray as some coastal species. It can grow up to 60 feet tall, but is usually shorter on the coast.

Juniper's appressed, scale-like leaves and pungent, light blue, berry-like cones are distinguishing characteristics. It has thin, stringy bark and a straight trunk. In exposed areas, however, Red Cedar becomes sculptured and quite flattened—stunted.

Juniper wood, both beautiful and durable, is highly valued, among other uses, for chest and cabinet making, fence posts, and boat construction. Along the Mid-Atlantic Coast, particularly in Maryland and Virginia, Red Cedar is heavily harvested for boat construction; there are not many big trees left. Most of the Chesapeake work boats are built of Juniper wood.

Red Cedar is found throughout the eastern half of the nation. Another closely related tree, Southern Red Cedar (*J. silicicola*), is distributed from southeastern Virginia to the Gulf Coast. One barrier island off the Eastern Shore of Virginia is called Cedar Island, and indeed the narrow maritime forest found there is dominated by this fragrant evergreen tree.

Part Two

Plants of Salt
and Brackish Marshes

SALT MARSHES ARE COASTAL WETLAND AREAS dominated by salt-loving (halophytic) grasses, particularly Saltmarsh Cordgrass. The marshes occur mainly in intertidal areas behind the barrier islands and barrier beaches that stretch along the Atlantic Coast.

Brackish marshes are coastal wetlands that are mainly grass dominated but that also support other vegetative forms such as sedges, rushes, and broad-leaved plants. They are found along the shorelines of estuaries and tidal rivers. The vegetation is more diverse because salinity has been reduced by mixing with fresh water.

Marshes develop through the accumulation of waterborne sediment. Marsh grasses propagate tidal flats by means of underground rhizomes. After the grasses become established, the marshes accumulate even more sediment because the grass plants themselves reduce water movement (tides and currents), and sediments fall out more rapidly. About half of the vegetation produced by a marsh remains within it, adding organic material to the sediments, allowing the marsh to build. The other half of the vegetative material is flushed into the water where it becomes the basis of the marine/estuarine food web.

Salt marshes in particular are laced with tidal creeks, channels, and guts. These waterways are havens for minnows such as mosquito minnows, killifish, silversides, as well as the young of sport and commercially important fish such as spot, croaker, and flounder.

Along the banks of the creeks and channels are literally thousands of tiny fiddler crabs that burrow into the mud of the marshes. Here also are the birds that eat these creatures—great blue herons, little green herons, bitterns, black crowned night herons, and various species of egrets and rails. This is also the haunt of the fish hawk or osprey.

The blue crab, a delicious and commercially important crustacean, is caught in the bays, lagoons, and tidal creeks of these marshes. Oysters and clams, perennial favorites for many seafood lovers, are particularly sought after because of their delicately salty flavor.

Perhaps one of the greatest wonders of these vast wetlands is the thousands of migratory waterfowl that fly in every year. Their sheer numbers and the din of their calls are mind boggling. The several large federal and state refuges along the Mid-Atlantic Coast are excellent places to observe the majestic flocks of Canada and snow geese and other waterfowl.

Salt and brackish marshes are important to the coastal estuarine and marine ecology. They both provide detritus to the system, the basis of the marine/estuarine food web as detailed in the Introduction. Not only do marshes export organic material to the estuary, but the estuary provides benefits to the marshes in the form of nutrients and sediment with each tidal cycle.

It is not just happenstance that the coastal aquatic system is rich with life. The estuaries benefit from the detritus produced by the marsh, the algae rich mud flats, and the seagrass beds in the shallows. In turn, these plant communities could not exist without the nutrient-rich estuarine and marine waters.

For many years, these wetlands were looked upon as wastelands. They were filled and built upon to accommodate the desires of people who wanted to live near the water. With the destruction of these natural areas and the eventual pollution from sewage and the other sources, the ecological integrity of the system was destroyed. Citizens began to realize that many of the things they had moved to the coast to enjoy were no longer there. As is often the case, the value of seemingly insignificant natural systems can seldom be overestimated, especially after they have been lost. The destruction of wetlands in most coastal states has been reduced, if not halted, in the last decade because of protective wetland laws. One hopes that these protective measures will continue to be successful.

Salt marshes in this region are well developed in Virginia and North Carolina. The intertidal portion of these southern marshes is usually more extensive than in the north. Above this zone, however, plant species composition is quite similar throughout the region, but there are exceptions. Meadow areas, largely dominated by Saltmeadow Hay, are more extensive in the north than they are in the southern part of the Bight. Meadows of this dense, wiry grass are flooded only during storms. Regular tides do not reach these high meadow marshes. Much of the detritus produced by Saltmeadow Hay remains within the marsh. The dense stands near the end of the growing season have a characteristic swirled or cowlick appearance. This is caused by the individual stems, which weaken by autumn and become entwined with one another when whipped by high winds and storms.

In New England as well as on Long Island and in New Jersey, a definite zone of Black Grass or Black Rush is typically found associated with the meadow. This small rush is replaced by Black Needlerush in the same general area of the marsh from Maryland and Virginia south. Although Black Rush is found as far south as Virginia it is seldom common there.

Salt Grass is frequently associated with Saltmeadow Hay in meadow areas, especially on lower, wetter, more saline sites and on the margins of depressions called pannes. Pannes are flooded during a storm surge or spring tide but do not drain completely on low tide. As the water evaporates, salinity concentrations increase, often to the level where nothing can grow. Many marshes are pockmarked with pannes that seldom support any type of vegetation.

Various associated species are found in the upper reaches of salt marshes as well. Sea Lavender, Sea Oxeye, Sea Blite, Orach, and three different species of Saltwort or Glasswort are found here. All of the species discussed thus far in this part are halophytes, vascular plants that can tolerate a highly saline environment.

At various distances from the ocean, one can find brackish marshes along the margins of estuaries and tidal rivers. Saltmarsh Cordgrass still dominates in the intertidal zone. However, above mean high water, brackish marsh species such as Big Cordgrass, Threesquare sedges, Narrow-leaved Cattail, Marsh Mallow, Water Hemp, Dwarf Spikerush, and Saltmarsh Bulrush are indicators of more moderate salinity levels.

These marshes are not only important to the estuarine environment but are also valuable to wildlife. Threesquare, Saltmarsh Bulrush, and cattails are highly attractive to muskrats for lodge construction and food. Seeds of Waterhemp and Saltmarsh Bulrush are prime food for waterfowl. These two species are often planted by hunt clubs and refuge managers to attract ducks and geese.

Some of the largest brackish marshes in this region are found along Chesapeake and Delaware bays and their tributaries, and along the sounds and tidal rivers of North Carolina. In addition to these large marshes, some more than four square miles in area, there are thousands of small marshes, many only a fraction of an acre in size. There is scientific evidence that even these small wetlands are important to the functional ecology of the estuary.

x ⅓

Saltmarsh Cordgrass
Smooth Cordgrass
Spartina alterniflora Loisel.

Saltmarsh Cordgrass is the dominant plant species of salt marshes on the Atlantic Coast. It comprises about 90 percent of these marshes. There are two easily recognized forms of this grass: the 4- to 7-foot-high *tall form* that is restricted to the margins of creeks, guts, natural channels, and other areas subject to daily tidal flooding, and the 1- to 2-foot-high *short form* that occupies the higher levels of the marsh near the upper limit of tidal influence. Both forms have relatively smooth leaves and culms. The leaves of the tall form range from 1/4 to 3/4 of an inch wide and up to 2 feet long, whereas in the short form the leaves are between 1/4 to 1/2 of an inch wide and range from 8 to 12 inches long. The tall form produces a long, narrow inflorescence in August. Its flowering head is actually a series of appressed branches that appear whitish-green in flower and tan in fruit. The short form seldom produces inflorescences. Although Saltmarsh Cordgrass produces seeds, its primary means of propagation is via rhizomes that send up young sprigs in adjacent tidal flats. The seeds are eaten by waterfowl in the fall and others are washed away by the tides. Those that remain lodged in the marsh above the high tide level have the potential of germinating in the spring.

Saltmarsh Cordgrass is an extremely hardy plant, able to tolerate tidal saltwater inundation and the fury of storm-lashed waters. No other species of higher plants can successfully compete with Cordgrass in this harsh environment except at the upper limits of its range (mean high water). Because of its tenaciousness, Cordgrass is valued for its ability to inhibit erosion. Waterfront property owners who have planted *S. alterniflora* within the intertidal zone of their shorelines are often rewarded, in time, by a fringing marsh that acts as a buffer to wave action. For a more detailed discussion on the value of Saltmarsh Cordgrass, refer to the Introduction.

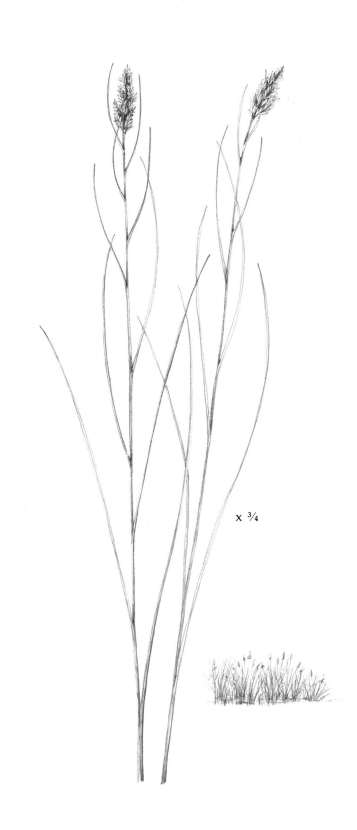

X ¾

Salt Grass
Distichlis spicata (L.) Greene

Salt Grass is one of the short (1 to 2 feet tall), wiry grasses that dominate the meadow community in higher parts of salt or brackish marshes. Salt Grass leaves are relatively short (1 to 5 inches), trough-shaped, and are arranged in one plane on opposite sides of the stem. The plant resembles Saltmeadow Hay, a grass that often grows with Salt Grass in the meadow community, but its leaves appear round and are arranged in several planes around the stem. The inflorescence of Salt Grass appears from August on as a densely compacted head, unlike the sparsely branched head of Saltmeadow Hay, which blooms earlier. The inflorescence of Salt Grass is whitish-green whereas Saltmeadow Hay heads are a rusty brown hue.

Salt Grass is usually found in the wetter, more saline parts of the meadow as it has the ability to withstand higher concentrations of salt than Saltmeadow Hay. It is often found along the margins of depressions or pannes in the meadows. Pannes typically fill with seawater during storms. They have no inlet or outlet, so as the water evaporates, its salinity increases. Salt Grass is often found in association with the short form of Saltmarsh Cordgrass, near or just above the mean high water line. In some cases, Salt Grass invades sand overwash areas or dredge spoil sites via its rhizomes, which send up young sprigs in a rope-like pattern.

Salt Grass ranges along the coast from the Maritimes to the Gulf of Mexico.

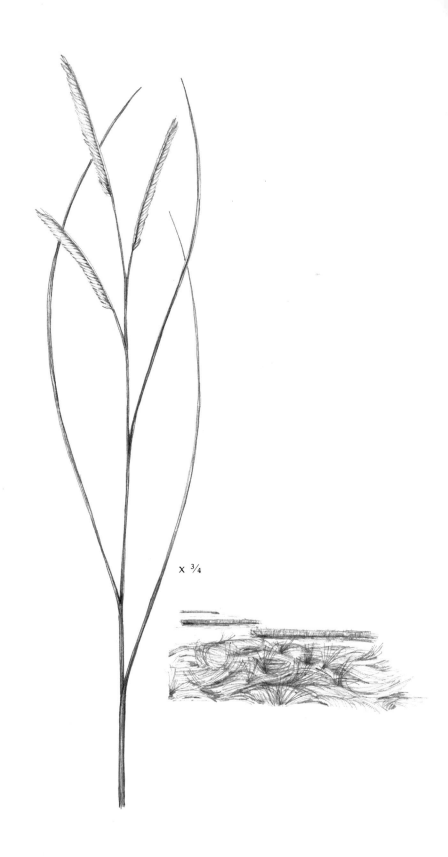

X ¾

Saltmeadow Hay
Spartina patens (Aiton) Muhl.

Saltmeadow Hay is a fine, wiry grass that appears collectively as a densely matted patch of meadow in the higher parts of salt or brackish marshes. It stands from 1-1/2 to 5 feet tall. The long tapering leaves are rolled inward and appear round. The longest leaves are nearly one-half or two-thirds the length of the stem. The base of the stem is weak and has a tendency to bend when stressed by winds or occasional spring tides. When this happens individual stems intertwine, and the overall effect is the characteristic cowlicks or swirls that often occur in large saltmarsh meadows. Sparingly branched, its heads appear brown in flower and fruit.

In lower areas in the meadow where water accumulates during spring tides, Saltmeadow Hay is often associated with Salt Grass. Towards the upper margin of the marsh, it is often found as a cover plant under Marsh Elder or Groundsel Tree. It also occurs on coastal sand dunes where it has a tufted growth form. Saltmeadow Hay is a common component of grassland communities typically found behind primary dunes.

The detritus produced by Saltmeadow Hay adds organic material to the marsh. It is not as dense as that of Saltmarsh Cordgrass, which can produce large rafts, and the young plants of Saltmeadow Hay have no trouble growing up through it in the spring.

In many marshes along the East Coast, Saltmeadow Hay is grazed or harvested as a forage crop for cattle. This grass is mainly a coastal species, ranging from Maine to Texas.

x ²⁄₃

Black Needlerush
Needle Rush
Juncus roemerianus Scheele

Black Needlerush is a stiff, coarse, and outwardly simple marsh rush, typically found growing in dense stands of nearly uniform heights of 2 to 5 feet. It is darker green than the typical saline marsh grass. The tip of the stem (actually a cylindrical leaf) has a noticeably sharp point from which its common name is derived.

The inflorescence of Black Needlerush is a cluster of tiny flowers that have a yellow-green cast. It is situated laterally on the stem, about three-quarters of the way up the stem. The flowering stage is illustrated.

Black Needlerush is usually found above the intertidal zone in brackish and saltwater marshes. The nearly black, coarse, rhizomes form dense mats that are resistant to erosion. *Juncus roemerianus* is most abundant throughout the South along the Atlantic Coastal Plain and the Gulf Coast to Texas.

Whereas Black Needlerush is common in the south, another rush, Black Grass or Black Rush (*J. gerardi*), is common in the northern saltmarshes. The ranges of these two species overlap in Maryland and Virginia. In this overlap zone one can easily distinguish Black Grass from Black Needlerush as the former is shorter and has a finer, more delicate appearance than the latter.

X ¾

Black Grass
Black Rush
Juncus gerardi Loisel.

Black Grass or Black Rush — the latter name is more appropriate because the plant is a true rush (Juncaceae) — is a common component of higher parts of salt and brackish marshes in the New England area. The stem and leaves are dark green, and a colony of Black Rush appears dark or nearly black at a distance, especially in contrast to the pea-green meadows where it is often found.

The fine, delicate stems of Black Rush are usually 1 to 3 feet tall with only one or two leaves, which are round in cross section. Its tiny yellow flowers occur in terminal, loose clusters. Black Rush propagates via seeds and slender rhizomes. Colonies result from vegetative progagation by rhizomes. The value of this plant lies mainly in its use as a cover for small animals and as a nesting place for rails. The flowering stage is pictured.

It ranges from Canada to Virginia, where it overlaps with another halophytic rush, Black Needlerush, a much taller, coarser, and more stiff plant than its northern counterpart. Black Rush and Black Needlerush occupy similar zones in saline marshes.

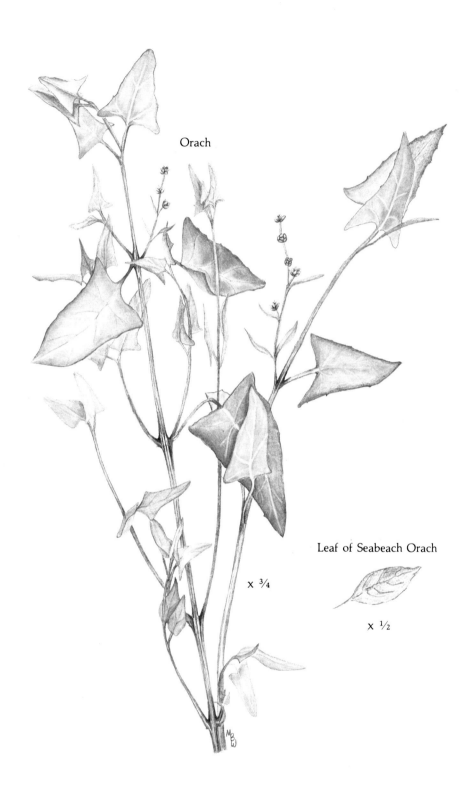

Orach

Leaf of Seabeach Orach

x $\frac{3}{4}$

x $\frac{1}{2}$

Orach

Spearscale
Atriplex patula L. var. *hastata* (L.) Gray
Seabeach Orach
Atriplex arenaria Nuttall

Orach is commonly found just above mean high water in salt and brackish marshes. It is regarded as an associated species, that is, Orach is almost never a major component of the saline marsh system. In the Mid-Atlantic region, the most common variety of this highly variable species is *Atriplex patula* var. *hastata* with its distinctive triangular leaves, hence the name Spearscale. The foliage has a pale gray-green appearance. The plant is lax and prostrate in appearance and in some cases grows like a vine. Its low-growing branches may extend three feet or more from the rooted main stem. Orach's small green flowers grow on the terminal part of its branches. They have no petals or sepals — only reproductive parts. The plant produces small, green, somewhat triangular fruit. It is an annual and reproduces via seeds. The seeds are eaten by birds.

Seabeach Orach (*Atriplex arenaria*), a close relative, occupies beach and dune habitats along the Atlantic Coast. It does not have the characteristic leaves of Spearscale, and its foliage has a pronounced mealy texture and appearance.

Spearscale and Seabeach Orach are found along the Atlantic Coast from New England to Florida.

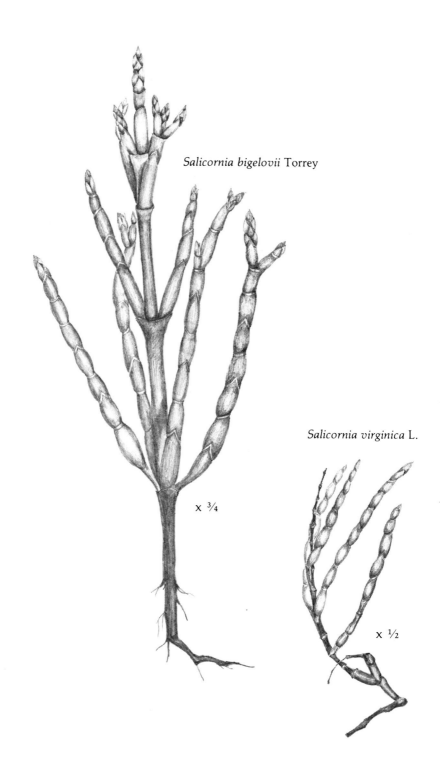

Salicornia bigelovii Torrey

Salicornia virginica L.

x ³⁄₄

x ¹⁄₂

Saltwort, Glasswort
Salicornia virginica L.
Salicornia europaea L.
Salicornia bigelovii Torrey

Some of the more unusual plants endemic in salt and brackish marshes are the Saltworts or Glassworts. Their thick green stems and succulent terminal branches are the color of jade. They stand from 6 inches to 2 feet tall. Wort is an old word for plant, hence salt plant. It is sometimes called Glasswort because the translucent stem resembles green glass. Saltwort's succulent stems have the ability to retain a relatively large volume of water compared to most plants. The stored water helps the plant to maintain a critical water balance, necessary because of the salty soil in which it grows. The physiology of the plant is such that it would have difficulty growing in non-saline areas.

These species of the genus *Salicornia* are flowering plants, essentially leafless. The flowers are inconspicuous and occur on the terminal portions of the branches.

Two species of *Salicornia*, *S. europaea* and *S. bigelovii*, are annuals, diffusely branched and fleshy. The perennial *Salicornia virginica* has hard or woody prostrate stems and is typically found in matted colonies. All three species commonly occur in the drier, sandy areas of the marsh. In salt marshes, *Salicornia virginica* is also found with the short form of Saltmarsh Cordgrass, *Spartina alterniflora*. *Salicornia europaea* turns to deep pink or ruby red in autumn; the other species turn brown or yellow.

The thick fleshy stems of all species can be pickled or preserved and are considered a delicacy.

All three species of *Salicornia* are found along the Atlantic, Gulf, and Pacific coasts.

X ³⁄₄

Marsh Fimbristylis
Fimbristylis spadicea (L.) Vahl.

This sedge is often found in, but is not limited to, the higher parts of brackish marshes along the Atlantic and Gulf coasts. The tall (1-1/2 to 2-1/2 feet), slender, rigid stem produces cylindrical, cone-like fruiting heads by late summer. The culm originates from a relatively dense tussock of basal leaves. Its flowers are inconspicuous; the clusters are very similar to fruiting heads, and it is nearly impossible to tell whether it is in flower or fruit without a hand lens. The leaves are round in cross section and about 1 to 1-1/2 feet long. This plant propagates by seed and vegetatively by rhizome.

Marsh Fimbristylis is often associated with Saltmeadow Hay and Salt Grass. Its stems, triangular in cross section, usually remain upright through the winter months. While *Fimbristylis* is seldom a dominant component of the high marsh area, at least several individuals are nearly always found in meadow areas in the southern part of the Mid-Atlantic region. The seeds are eaten by waterfowl.

Limonium nashii Small

x ⅓

Sea Lavender

Limonium carolinianum (Walter) Britton
Limonium nashii Small

Sea Lavenders are perennial herbs with basal rosettes of fleshy, leathery, smooth leaves and diffusely spreading inflorescences (panicles) dotted with a multitude of tiny lavender or blue flowers. The panicles are prized for bouquets and dried arrangements. They are commonly found in salt or brackish marshes but are seldom a dominant part of the marsh community. The leafy rosette of the plant is 2 to 4 inches high and 4 to 8 inches wide. The flower stem grows 1-1/2 to 2-1/2 feet tall.

The two different species of Sea Lavenders occurring along the Atlantic and Gulf coasts—*Limonium carolinianum* and *Limonium nashii*—are almost identical in appearance. Only after close examination of the tiny blossoms can one differentiate between the two.

Sea Lavenders bloom from July to October (as illustrated), and their leaves remain until mid-winter. As with most saline marsh plants, these species are halophytic, tolerant of salt water. Sea Lavender is a perennial, it has a vertical taproot, and it propagates by seeds. It has lignin (a woody substance) in its epidermal cell walls; there is some speculation that this has protective value in the saline environment.

x 1

Sea Oxeye
Borrichia frutescens (L.) DC.

Sea Oxeye, a low (1 to 2 feet tall), shrubby, halophytic perennial with thick (1/16 to 1/8 of an inch), fleshy leaves, is often found in dense colonies in high marsh areas. Endemic to southern salt or brackish marshes, it ranges from Virginia to the Gulf Coast. Flowering in mid-summer, Sea Oxeye's yellow, daisy-like blossoms stand out in the green carpet landscape of the marshes. *Borrichia* is often associated with Saltmeadow Hay and is frequently found on the fringes of saltbush communities.

A dark brown, rosette of bur-like seed heads appears in late autumn. However, the most common means of propagation is by underground rhizomes, resulting in characteristic clone populations. Pictured is the stem in flower.

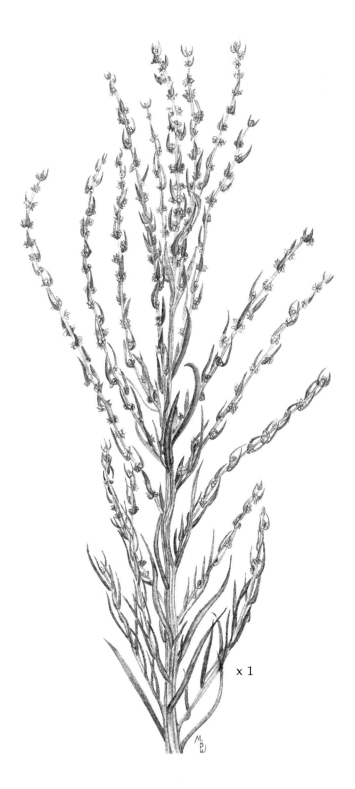

x 1

Sea Blite
Suaeda linearis (Ell.) Moq.

Sea Blite is a tall (1-1/2 to 2-1/2 feet), erect plant with many fleshy, linear leaves on a single, branching stem. The leaves are alternate, 1/2 to 1-1/4 inches long, and are appressed on the top three-quarters of the plant. They are somewhat succulent, retaining water for regulating the osmotic pressure, an adaptive mechanism in saline environments. The plant grows singly or in sparse clumps. The flowering stage is illustrated.

Sea Blite is found in salt or brackish marshes, is often associated with Saltwort, and may be found interspersed with sparse Saltmarsh Cordgrass populations. In late summer or early fall, numerous tiny (1/8 of an inch wide) green flowers are produced on the top one-third of the plant. This annual plant is shallow-rooted and is propagated by seeds. Its seeds are eaten by birds.

Sea Blite ranges throughout the Atlantic and Gulf coasts. Its habitats vary from wet with Saltmarsh Cordgrass to relatively dry with *Salicornia*.

X ¾

Saltmarsh Aster
Aster tenuifolius L.

In early summer, the foliage of Saltmarsh Aster is difficult to distinguish within its habitat of dense stands of marsh grass, especially in colonies of Saltmarsh Cordgrass. Later in the season, however, white or faintly magenta blooms appear. The long, narrow leaves are alternate, somewhat succulent, and adhere to the stem for about one-third of its length, which varies from 1 to 3-1/2 feet. This plant is a perennial and produces slender, creeping rhizomes.

Saltmarsh Aster is known as an associated species, that is, a plant that is never abundant in plant communities but is likely to be associated with the dominant species of a given community — in this case Saltmarsh Cordgrass.

Aster tenuifolius is seldom common or abundant throughout its range, which extends along the Atlantic Coast from Massachusetts to Louisiana on the Gulf Coast. A very similar species, *Aster subulatus*, occurs within this same range but occupies tidal freshwater marshes. *Aster subulatus* is more robust (leafier and more branched) than *Aster tenuifolius*. It is also an annual whereas Saltmarsh Aster is a perennial.

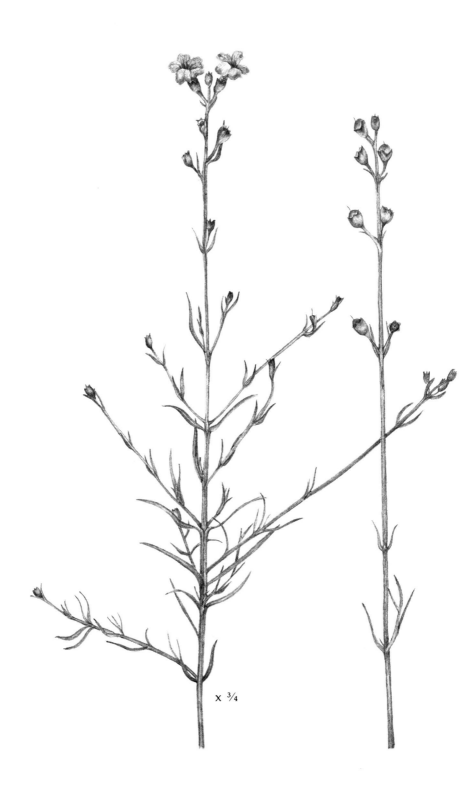

X ¾

Maritime Gerardia
Agalinis maritima (Raf.) Raf.

The attractive herb Maritime Gerardia with its rose or magenta flowers is found only rarely or occasionally in salt marshes of the Mid-Atlantic region. It has narrow, succulent leaves and smooth, erect stems. Maritime Gerardia usually grows 1 to 3 feet tall in colonies of several individuals in the meadow (Saltmeadow Hay) areas of a salt marsh. The magenta petals of the flower are fused into a tube that has yellow and purple markings within. A close inspection of the flowers of this plant is certainly worthwhile. Because of their rarity in the region, these plants should not be disturbed.

Gerardia is distributed from Nova Scotia to Texas in salt marshes along the coast but is found only as a few scattered colonies of individuals throughout its range. The fruit and flower stage is depicted. An annual Maritime Gerardia propagates only by seed.

X ¾

Marsh Pink
Sea Pink
Sabatia stellaris Pursh

One of the more delightful herbs found in salt or brackish marshes is Marsh Pink. Neither abundant nor rare, it has an appeal about it that makes one wonder if it is an escapee from a flower garden.

Each flower has 5 (usually) pink petals and a bright yellow center. Flower color may vary in this plant from white to lilac to pink, but the center is always yellow. It flowers from July through September. The leaves are set opposite each other on the branched stem and are broad on the lower part of the plant and narrow (linear) near the apex. Marsh Pink is found in the higher parts of coastal saline marshes and is commonly associated with Saltmeadow Hay, Sea Oxeye, Sea Lavender, and Salt Grass. It is an annual and propagates only via seeds. Sea Pink ranges along the Atlantic Coast from Massachusetts to Florida.

x 1

Saltmarsh Loosestrife
Lythrum lineare L.

Saltmarsh Loosestrife can be found in salt or brackish marshes from Long Island to Texas. Its habitat is in the meadow areas with Salt-meadow Hay or in the upper part of the intertidal zone with Saltmarsh Cordgrass. The plant is most obvious by mid-summer when it has matured to its fullest extent, up to 3 feet tall, and thereby stands above most of the shorter marsh grasses. At this stage it is a multi-branched herb with small linear leaves about 1/8 of an inch wide and small white or bluish-white blooms. The leaves are usually but not always opposite and are 1/2 to 2 inches long. The stem is smooth and angular. Saltmarsh Loosestrife is seldom abundant or common in saline marshes and is more likely to be seen in the southern part of the Mid-Atlantic region. A perennial, Loosestrife often comes up in the same area of a marsh year after year, but colonies are made up of only a few individual plants. It propagates by both rhizomes and seeds. The mature plant in flower is drawn.

X ¾

Marsh Elder
Gall Bush
Iva frutescens L.

Marsh Elder is found at the upland margins or on small hummocks in salt or brackish marshes. It seldom grows over 10 feet tall and has opposite deciduous leaves. The leaves are thick (1/16 of an inch), have serrated margins, and taper towards both ends. They range from 1 to 3-1/2 inches long. Marsh Elder belongs to the Compositae family. The chief characteristic of this family is that its flowers are diminutive and are compactly arranged in heads (composites). In Marsh Elder, the flower head is surrounded by a series of tiny, green, leaf-like appendages called an involucre. Many flower heads of Marsh Elder are arranged on terminal stems and appear as green globular fruits. The illustration shows these globular flowering heads.

Marsh Elder often occurs with another shrub, Groundsel Tree, to form the saltbush community at higher levels in the marsh, usually near the upland border. The two shrubs are similar in appearance, but a closer look will reveal characteristic differences. Groundsel Tree's thinner leaves are alternately arranged. The leaves of Marsh Elder are oppositely arranged and are more regularly toothed. The blades also taper towards both ends. Marsh Elder ranges from the Maritime Provinces to Florida on the Atlantic Coast and to Texas on the Gulf Coast.

X ³⁄₄

Groundsel Tree
Silvering
Sea Myrtle
Consumption Weed
Baccharis halimifolia L.

Groundsel Tree is a tall, robust shrub that may grow to a height of more than 15 feet. It has thin, alternate leaves. The upper leaves are small (1/2 to 1 inch long) and lack teeth, whereas the lower leaves are longer (1-1/2 to 2-1/2 inches long), wedge-shaped, and have long, irregular teeth. The shrub is dioecious, that is, an individual shrub may have either female (pistillate) or male (staminate) blossoms, but not both. In late August or September, the beige-yellow flower heads appear, and by late September and until early winter the white bristles on the seeds of the pistillate shrubs are prominent. The illustration shows the shrub in summer budding stage. Although Groundsel Tree is deciduous, the naked stems remain slightly green throughout the winter. In contrast, the bare branches of Marsh Elder have a light gray appearance. In the summer, thin alternate leaves distinguish Groundsel Tree from Marsh Elder with its thick, opposite, regularly toothed leaves.

Groundsel Tree is often associated with Marsh Elder to form what is collectively known as the saltbush community, located in the high parts of salt or brackish marshes usually at the marsh/upland border. They are known as saltbushes because they are found in saline marshes. Saltbushes are collectors of flotsam — timber, eel grass, crab pot floats, and other debris left by floodwaters.

Groundsel Tree has a number of regional common names: Silvering (because of its white seeds), Sea Myrtle, and Consumption Weed, to name a few.

This shrub is mainly a coastal species, ranging from Massachusetts to Florida and throughout the Gulf Coast.

American Threesquare

Olney Threesquare

x 1

Olney Threesquare
Scirpus olneyi Gray
American Threesquare
Chairmaker's Rush
Scirpus americanus Persoon

Olney Threesquare (2 to 5 feet tall) and American Threesquare (2 to 6 feet tall) are distinct from any other grass-like plants of brackish or freshwater marshes. Both sedges have triangular stems in cross-section and have few if any stem leaves at maturity. The seed clusters appear to extend laterally from the stem near the apex.

Although the two species are similar, there are distinguishing differences. Olney Threesquare usually grows in more saline environments than does American Threesquare, and its seed clusters are situated closer to the apex. A closer look at the seed clusters of the two species (by use of a hand lens) reveals more detailed differences in the scales that subtend the clusters. The scales of *Scirpus americanus* have a characteristically notched apex and a minute, needle-like extension, whereas the scales of *Scirpus olneyi* have a broad, obtuse apex.

American Threesquare is also known as Chairmaker's Rush. In the past it was used for caning chair seats. Today craftsmen get their weaving materials from supply houses; most of these materials are plant fibers from the tropics.

The seeds of these sedges are eaten by waterfowl. The stems are used by muskrats in lodge construction.

S. olneyi is mainly a coastal sedge; *S. americanus* ranges throughout much of the continental United States as well as coastal wetlands. The Threesquares grow in various parts of the marsh but seem to do well where they are reached by tides. The fruiting stage is illustrated. Threesquares propagate by both seeds and rhizomes.

x ½

Saltmarsh Bulrush
Threesquare
Scirpus robustus Pursh

As the scientific name suggests, this 4- to 6-foot-tall sedge is robust, both in stature and in its development of a large cluster of brown seed heads in late summer. It is often called Threesquare because of its stem, triangular in cross section. However, unlike the other Threesquare commonly found in low salinity marshes, Saltmarsh Bulrush has a number of prominent stem leaves. Olney Threesquare and American Threesquare have very few leaves, and these typically disappear late in the growing season.

The lustrous brown seeds of Saltmarsh Bulrush are a favorite food of waterfowl. Also important are its stems and leaves as they are used by muskrats to build their lodges. For these reasons, Saltmarsh Bulrush is often planted to improve waterfowl and wildlife habitats.

Saltmarsh Bulrush grows primarily but not exclusively in intertidal areas. It reproduces vegetatively by rhizomes and by seeds. It ranges from Nova Scotia to Florida on the Atlantic Coast and from Florida to Texas on the Gulf Coast.

X ³/₄

Saltmarsh Foxtail Grass
Setaria geniculata (Lam.) Beauvois

This short (1 to 2 feet tall), coarse grass with its bristly head is often found in the higher parts of coastal marshes, on low dunes, and in disturbed areas such as roadsides that cut through meadows. It grows in clumps, usually with only a few individual plants, and propagates by both seeds and rhizomes. Its leaves are green with a purple tinge.

Though not strictly a salt marsh halophyte, for it is found throughout much of the interior of the eastern part of the country, Saltmarsh Foxtail Grass does tolerate saltwater intrusion. It is occasionally associated with Saltmeadow Hay, Sea Oxeye, and Marsh Elder. Although this species is more common in the southern part of the Mid-Atlantic region, it has been found as far north as New England. The most distinctive characteristic of Saltmarsh Foxtail Grass is its spike-like, bristly head, green during the flowering stage and tawny when seeds develop. Birds eat its seeds. The fruiting stage is drawn.

X ¾

Saltmarsh Fleabane
Camphorweed
Pluchea purpurascens (Swartz) DC.

This pink-flowered plant is often found near the lower limit of the Salt Grass meadow areas of brackish marshes, above the tide zone. Saltmarsh Fleabane's tiny flowers are concentrated into flower heads that bloom from late July through October. The entire plant, especially the leaves, is pubescent (downy). Though the tiny short hairs can only be seen with a 10× hand lens, the leaves feel downy or velvety to the touch. The leaves are lance-shaped, alternate, and have serrated edges. The plant has a slight medicinal smell, hence the epithet Camphorweed.

Saltmarsh Fleabane plants grow to 3 feet high and form a striking contrast with the flat, low appearance of the saltmeadows. Saltmeadows are meadow areas in a salt marsh that are vegetated by Saltmeadow Hay or Salt Grass or both.

Another species, *Pluchea foetida*, is similar to Saltmarsh Fleabane except that it has white or cream-colored flowers and is less common. Both plants have a peculiar odor that reportedly repels insects, and both are members of the Compositae family.

Saltmarsh Fleabane and *Pluchea foetida* are found chiefly along the Atlantic and Gulf coasts. Saltmarsh Fleabane rarely produces rhizomes and propagates chiefly by seeds. The flowering stage is illustrated.

X ¾

Marsh Mallow
Seashore Mallow
Kosteletzkya virginica (L.) Persl.

Marsh Mallow, a leafy, 2- to 3-foot-tall herb, is often found in
brackish or tidal freshwater marshes. Its most striking feature is its
large (1 to 3 inches) pink blooms that come out in late July and
August. Both the stems and the foliage of Marsh Mallow are rough to
the touch, a texture caused by minute, dense, stellate (star-shaped)
hairs or protrusions visible only with a $10\times$ to $20\times$ hand lens. The
lower stem leaves are lobed and resemble maple leaves. Its habitats
are various—in saltmeadows and with Marsh Elder usually, but not
always, in higher parts of the marsh. It propogates by both seed and
rhizome.

This species should not be confused with the true Marsh Mallow,
Althaea officinalis. During colonial times a confection was made from
a mucilaginous substance extracted from the roots of *Althaea*, hence
the marshmallow of today. *Althaea* is velvety to the touch and each
flower has many styles whereas *Kosteletzkya* is coarse to the touch
and the flowers have only five styles. *Kosteletzkya* is a coastal species
ranging from Long Island to the Gulf of Mexico.

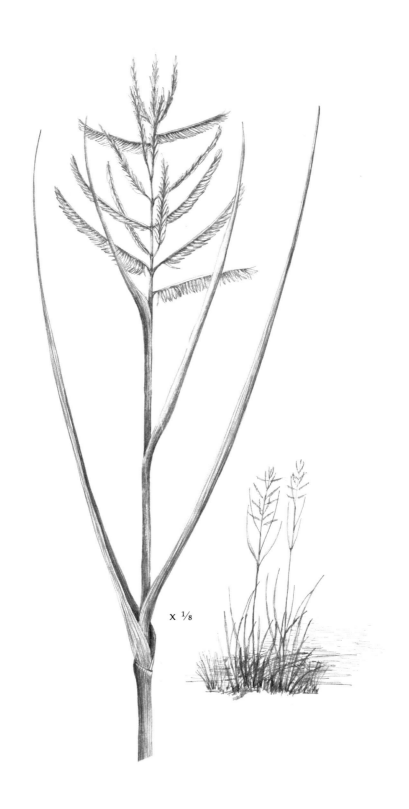

x ¹⁄₈

Big Cordgrass
Spartina cynosuroides (L.) Roth

Big Cordgrass is the largest of the *Spartina* marsh grasses, often attaining heights of 12 feet or more in low salinity marshes. This coarse perennial frequently grows in dense, monospecific stands along tidal rivers that may extend 50 miles or more inland from the Atlantic. This majestic grass often forms a tall border along the marsh/upland ecotone of salt marshes. Its 6- to 12-inch branching inflorescence turns from green to tan when in seed. It propagates by both seed and rhizome.

The leaves of Big Cordgrass are arranged on the stem in overlapping sheaths, the leaves coming off in different directions. These long tapering leaves have minute upturned teeth along their margins. Despite these knife-like blades, which can scratch or cut the skin, Big Cordgrass is often used by duck hunters as camouflage for duck blinds.

The long, stout rhizomes of this grass are a favorite food for geese, who dig them. Muskrats use the foliage and stems for lodge construction. The illustration shows the plant in seed.

Big Cordgrass is found in tidal waters from New England to the Gulf Coast.

x ½

Waterhemp
Amaranthus cannabinus (L.) J. D. Sauer.

Waterhemp is a tall, robust (leafy, producing many flowers and fruits), willowy annual that reaches heights of 8 feet or more. *A. cannabinus* is most common in brackish water and low salinity marshes. As the scientific name suggests, the overall appearance of the plant resembles that of Hemp, *Cannabis sativa*; however, the resemblance ends there. The simple, narrow, willow-like leaves of Waterhemp cannot be mistaken for the characteristic compound leaves of *Cannabis*.

In a typical coastal marsh dominated by grasses, sedges, and rushes, the young plants of Waterhemp are not usually seen during the early part of the growing season. By late summer, however, the tree-like growth habit (a single stem with many branches) is obvious. When the plant is nearly mature, a profusion of small, green or yellow flowers is produced on leafy spikes or panicles, as pictured. By fall a single large plant may produce a quart of seeds, an important food for waterfowl. Waterhemp is sometimes planted in marshes by wildlife managers and duck hunters to attract ducks and geese.

Waterhemp ranges from Maine to Florida along the Atlantic Coast. An annual, it reproduces only by seed.

X ¾

Germander
Wood Sage
Teucrium canadense L. var. *canadense*

This variety of Germander, which stands 2 to 3 feet tall, is occasionally seen in drier, higher areas of low saline and freshwater marshes along the coast from Maine to Florida. While not rare, Germander is seldom abundant in any given marsh. It propagates by both seed and rhizome.

Germander is a member of the mint family (Labiatae). Other species within this family have long been used as flavoring agents or for medicinal purposes and are commonly cultivated. Although this species does not have any of these values to my knowledge, it is easily recognized as a mint because of its stem (square in cross-section), opposite leaves, and characteristic flowers. Flower color varies and may be purple, blue, pink, or white. The leaves are hairy or even velvet-like underneath. Though some people cannot detect it, Germander has a faint sage odor when crushed.

Part Three

Plants of
Freshwater Wetlands,
Tidal and Nontidal

LUXURIANT AND COLORFUL, tidal freshwater marshes and swamps often exist in some of the more remote areas on the coast. Nearly all of these wetlands are riverine. The water rises and falls in response to oceanic lunar tides, but the differences in tidal period may be six or seven hours or more between the ocean itself and the upper limits of tidal action, known as the fall line. The surge of fresh water from interior sources is stronger than saline water movement, but it cannot overcome the influence of tide.

Tidal fluctuation has an influence on plant zonation. The intertidal zone is characterized by two species of fleshy-leaved plants, Arrow Arum and Pickerelweed. This plant community is very dense. The broad, fleshy leaves of these two species may be up to 2 feet long and more than 3 feet long. At the peak of the growing season these two species give the marsh a tropical-like appearance. This zone is distinctive, both from the ground and from the air. The broadleaved species (Arrow Arum and Pickerelweed) contrast with the upper part of the marsh (above mean high water) where there is a mixture of grasses, sedges, rushes, and various other species with less luxuriant foliage. In a broad sense, these large succulent plants with their generous leaves are ecological equivalents of Saltmarsh Cordgrass as they both occupy the same zone. Yellow Pond Lily or Spatter Dock is usually found in the lower part of this zone. The fleshy leaves float on the water surface at high tide and droop somewhat at low tide but remain above the water.

The higher parts of these marshes are usually the most extensive and the most complex. Communities in this area are difficult to classify because of both density and diversity of vegetation.

One of the most delicate and yet most majestic grasses in the coastal zone is Northern Wild Rice. Its lacey, yellowish flowering heads and broad, sword-like leaves are distinctive in these marshes, even at a distance. The seeds (grains) of this plant and a number of other species make these wetlands highly attractive to waterfowl.

Beavers frequently dam the upper reaches of tidal swamps. Muskrat populations are so dense in some marshes that their grassy lodges appear as a field of miniature haystacks. These grassy, hut-like dwellings average six or more per acre in productive wetlands.

Vegetational variations with the seasons are much more explicit than in salt or brackish marshes. The freshwater marsh appears to be nothing more than a mud flat in winter. This is particularly true in the intertidal zone. The foliage of Arrow Arum and Pickerelweed decays rapidly at the end of the growing season. The once luxuriant, tropical-like foliage is gone by mid-winter, and only small humps are discernible beneath the mud surface. These are harbingers of things to come, underground rhizomes that will shoot up new foliage in the spring. An observer in these marshes in April or May, depending on the latitude within the region, would note that the wetland, with few exceptions, remains a mud flat. Wild Rice patches look like plowed fields, the result of geese and ducks digging and eating the rhizomes over the winter. Most of the rice grains are long gone, either eaten by redwinged blackbirds in early autumn or perhaps by early arrivals of migratory waterfowl. Some grains, however, are germinating in the mud. What is left of this once magnificent stand is an amorphic mass of naked fruiting heads, frayed and partially decayed foliage, and pieces of rhizomes. Seeds and rhizomes that escape the winter feast will generate new plants. By September, yellow-green heads will sway in the wind, and again the grand embarkation will begin somewhere in Canadian wetlands.

Our observer will also note rather strange spike-like projections in the intertidal zone. These structures are actually the sprigs of Arrow Arum, tightly layered and enrolled young leaves that unfold as temperatures increase.

Vernal sedges of the genus *Carex* appear now in thick green tufts or clumps, but the dominant vegetation in spring is still the broad-leaved species, Arrow Arum and Pickerelweed.

The diversity of the marsh is noteworthy by August, by which time one easily finds thirty to fifty species of plants in a given marsh. Here are found colorful plants such as the purple flowered Ironweed standing up to 8 feet tall, Marsh Hibiscus with white blooms up to 6 inches across, the bright yellow blooms of Beggar's Ticks and Sneezeweed, the unusual orange flowers of Jewelweed, the brilliant Cardinal Flower, and many others.

A number of herbs are not as appealing but nevertheless have value as waterfowl food. Walter's Millet, so heavily laden with seeds, weakens and lies on the marsh surface. The small grains of this grass are relished by ducks and geese in the fall. The tiny seeds of Smartweeds, Tearthumbs, and Water Dock are also eaten by migratory waterfowl as well as by resident marsh birds. Wildlife managers and hunt clubs often sow seeds of the above species as well as those of Threesquare, Saltmarsh Bulrush, and Waterhemp in order to attract waterfowl.

Tidal freshwater swamps prevail along many tidal rivers of the coastal plain. In North Carolina and Virginia, coastal swamps are dominated by Bald Cypress, Red Maple, Black Gum, and Tupelo Gum. Tupelo Gum is more common in North Carolina than in

Virginia. Associated trees are Swamp Cottonwood, ashes, and Sweet Bay. From Maryland north, the most common trees in these wetland areas are Red Maple, Black Gum, Atlantic White Cedar, River Birch, and Black Willow. Bald Cypress extends north into Maryland and into one or two isolated areas in Delaware, but it is not common except in the southern tributaries of Chesapeake Bay. Shrubs such as Sweetpepper Bush, Buttonbush, Swamp Dogwood, and Alder often form a border along the tidal banks under the trees.

Many species found in the marsh are also found under the swamp canopy, though their diversity and density is reduced because of shading. Swamp trees often invade marshes, and if succession is not interrupted, certain marsh areas will become swamps. Red Maple appears to be the principal pioneer invader of marshes.

x ½

Pickerelweed
Tuckahoe
Pontederia cordata L.

Pickerelweed (2 to 4 feet tall) often grows in association with Arrow Arum in the intertidal zone of freshwater marshes. Both plants have fleshy leaves that emerge from underground rhizomes. The leaves of Pickerelweed are heart-shaped and have an array of veins closely paralleling the general shape of the leaf. These leaves are 8 to 15 inches long and 4 to 7 inches wide. Arrow Arum has larger, triangular-shaped leaves with three dominant and many subordinate veins.

Pickerelweed's inflorescence is a spike of blue flowers subtended by a single leaf-like bract. During the blooming season, which may extend from May until October, a marsh dominated by this plant will have a characteristic blue hue, contrasting with the dark green of its foliage. During the winter, however, the above-ground portion of these plants quickly decomposes, leaving only bare mud flats. Pickerelweed is a perennial. It can propagate by seed, but plants come up yearly from the rhizomes.

Pickerelweed serves as a food source for several species of wildlife. The sticky red seeds are eaten by ducks, and the thick, short rhizomes are eaten by muskrats.

Pickerelweed ranges throughout the eastern United States in wetland areas.

X ¼

Arrow Arum
Duck Corn
Peltandra virginica (L.) Kunth

Arrow Arum or Duck Corn is an emergent, fleshy perennial found in the intertidal areas of freshwater marshes. (An emergent plant is an aquatic plant that is rooted in the underwater substrate but whose leaves and flowers emerge above the water.) It is often associated with Pickerelweed. Its dominant characteristics are the large triangular leaf blades (up to 3 feet long) and the pod-like fruiting heads. Arrow Arum grows in dense clumps with leaf stalks (originating from rhizomes) that attain heights of 3 to 7 feet. Not necessarily a coastal plant, Arrow Arum is found in wetland areas throughout the southeastern part of the country.

In late May or June, an elongated, leaf-like, reproductive appendage develops. It resembles a pointed rolled leaf (spathe), and it surrounds a fleshy, cylindrical inflorescence (spadix). These are characteristic features of the Araceae family to which Arrow Arum belongs, as does Sweet Flag, another freshwater marsh plant. Arrow Arum's inflorescence is long and pointed as depicted in the upper left of the drawing; the fruiting pod is on the right. As the fruits develop, the tip of the spathe decays, leaving a pod-like fruiting head.

During late summer and early autumn, the inflorescence is transformed into a pod-like seed case which droops to the marsh mud and decays, eventually releasing seeds. The fleshy dark-green to black seeds (3/8 of an inch in diameter) are distributed by the tides for many miles. The oxalic acid content of Arrow Arum seeds is high; only Wood Ducks eat them regularly. In the spring of the year, the seeds from the previous fall secrete a clear gelatinous mass that often attains the size of a golf ball. This mass may aid in propagation by preventing dessication and by aiding in buoyancy.

Arrow Arum is found throughout the eastern United States in wetland areas.

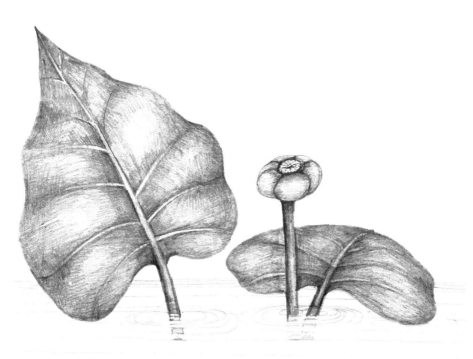

X ¹⁄₄

Yellow Pond Lily
Spatter Dock
Nuphar luteum (L.) Sibthrop & Smith

Yellow Pond Lily is a perennial commonly found in nontidal standing water or in tidal freshwater marshes. It produces a bulbous flower with thick, succulent sepals and many yellow petals. In tidal waters, the leaves are emergent at low tide and often float on a high tide. The leaves vary from nearly round to heart-shaped, and they grow up to 1 foot wide and 1-1/2 to 2 feet long. The leaves are pinnately veined; that is, one central vein with secondary veins coming off at right angles. Both leaves and flower stalks originate from stout rhizomes embedded in the muddy bottom. Depending on water depth or tidal range, these stalks can be anywhere from 2 to 5 feet long. In nontidal waters, the leaves nearly always float. The leaves and flower stalks decay and decompose rapidly in autumn; by December only the rhizomes of these colonies are left, embedded in the mud below the water surface.

Yellow Pond Lily provides cover for fishes and attachment sites for small aquatic animals and algae. This plant ranges through much of the eastern and midwestern United States. It is found throughout the Mid-Atlantic coastal region. Drawn are the leaves and the flower in bloom.

x ½

Bultongue
Sagittaria falcata Pursh

Bultongue, *Sagittaria falcata,* is closely related to Arrowhead, *Sagittaria latifolia.* Their flowers are similar but their leaf characteristics are different. Arrowhead leaves are shaped like arrowheads, while Bultongue leaves are lance-shaped, hence the name Bultongue.

The stems arise from rhizomes. The plant can be either emergent or on the marsh surface with no water. The inflorescence grows to 3 feet tall. Its leaves are 1-1/2 to 2-1/2 feet long, and the blades are 2 to 5 inches wide and 8 to 12 inches long. Each flower has 3 white petals around a yellow center. The drawing depicts the plant in fruit — the petals have fallen. Bultongue propagates by seeds.

This plant is distributed along the Atlantic and Gulf coasts from Delaware to Texas. Bultongue appears to be the most common *Sagittaria* found in tidal freshwater wetlands in the southern part of the Mid-Atlantic Coast. Bultongue is often associated with Pickerelweed and Arrow Arum in the intertidal zone of coastal marshes, but is seldom abundant as are the other two species.

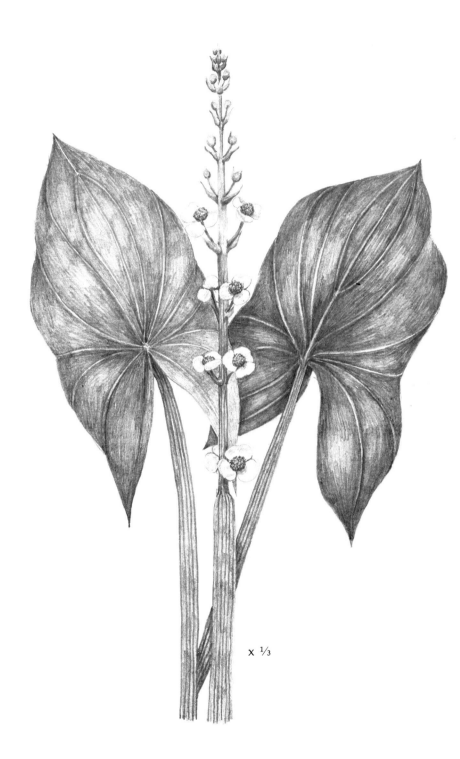

x ⅓

Arrowhead
Duck Potato
Sagittaria latifolia Willd.

Arrowhead, typically a 2- to 3-foot-tall emergent plant, is frequently found in tidal freshwater marshes in the intertidal zone, where it is often associated with Arrow Arum and Pickerelweed. Its large fleshy leaves are shaped like arrowheads. The leaves are highly variable in size, ranging from very slender to very broad (up to 2 feet wide), but the arrowhead shape remains constant. All species belonging to this genus have flower stalks that produce white tripetalate flowers with yellow staminate and pistillate centers.

The name Duck Potato is derived from the fact that bulbs produced on the ends of underground rhizomes are dug up and eaten by waterfowl. As a matter of fact, Arrowhead tubers are quite fit for human consumption, but they are hard to find in the mud and are seldom larger than a golf ball.

Arrowhead is found the length of the Atlantic coast as well as in wetland areas inland. It reproduces by both seed and bulb. The drawing depicts Arrowhead in flower.

x 1/8

American Lotus
Lotus Lily
Nelumbo lutea (Willd.) Persoon

The only lotus native to the North American continent deserves to be included in this book if for no other reason than its majestic beauty. American Lotus is an aquatic freshwater plant with very large (2 or more feet in diameter) round leaves and huge pale yellow blooms up to 8 inches wide. The disc-like leaves are unusual not only because of their size and shape, but also because their leaf stalks are attached to the centers of the blades.

The leaves and flowers of this plant may extend 3 feet above the water; the entire length of leaves and flowering stems (both under water and above) may be as much as 6 feet.

Late in the season, the American Lotus plant produces a large cone-shaped fruiting receptacle in which are embedded acorn-like seeds. The receptacle is often used in dried arrangements. The seeds have a hard, dark brown outer shell, but the meat inside is white and edible. Its flavor is similar to that of the chestnut.

Along certain parts of the Mississippi and Illinois river systems and in some areas in the southeastern United States, American Lotus is viewed as an obnoxious weed because it clogs waterways to the point that boats cannot pass through. Though found throughout the Mid-Atlantic Coast, its abundance is variable. It is abundant in certain river systems in Maryland, but is found only occasionally in Virginia. It is a weed in some river systems in North Carolina.

Broad-leaved Cattail   Narrow-leaved Cattail

x ½   x ½

Cattail
Narrow-leaved Cattail
Typha angustifolia L.
Broad-leaved Cattail
Common Cattail
Typha latifolia L.

The two most common Cattails found in East Coast tidal marshes, brackish and freshwater, are the Narrow-leaved and Broad-leaved cattails.

Typha angustifolia, the Narrow-leaved Cattail, is commonly found in brackish and freshwater marshes. It has narrow leaves (about 1/4 to 1/2 of an inch wide), and the characteristic flower spike has a distinct gap between the upper, male portion (staminate) and the lower, female (pistillate) portion. In brackish marshes, Narrow-leaved Cattails are typically found in dense colonies along the upland margin where there is freshwater seepage.

The Broad-leaved Cattail, *Typha latifolia*, is more common in freshwater marshes. This species has no (or only a slight) gap between the staminate and pistillate portions of the spike and has leaves up to 1-1/2 inches wide. Both species are common in various types of wetlands, especially where there is standing water, throughout much of North America.

In the spring, the young emerging Cattail plant can be eaten. Slightly later in the season, in late April or early May, the tender developing spike is also edible. It reaches full development by June. After the flower spike is mature (after it extends above the leaves), it becomes tough and inedible. Many people consider the young plant and its tender spike to be delicacies. The rootstocks of both species are eaten by geese and muskrats.

x ¹/₂

Lizard's Tail

Saururus cernuus L.

Lizard's Tail is a curious wetland plant, distinctive when in flower. Its generic name comes from the Greek words *sauros* (lizard) and *oura* (tail), which refer to its elongated, white-flowering spike. Also distinctive are its heart-shaped leaves.

Lizard's Tail often grows in the intertidal zone of freshwater marshes and swamps as well as in ditches and on the edges of ponds and small streams. In these habitats it is usually associated with Pickerelweed, Arrow Arum, and Arrowhead, although it is seldom the predominant species. It grows 2 to 3 feet tall, and its leaves are 3 to 6 inches long and 2 to 4 inches wide. It propagates by both seeds and rhizomes. The drawing depicts the plant as it would be seen June through August.

Saururus is found in freshwater wetlands throughout much of the eastern United States and throughout the Mid-Atlantic Coast.

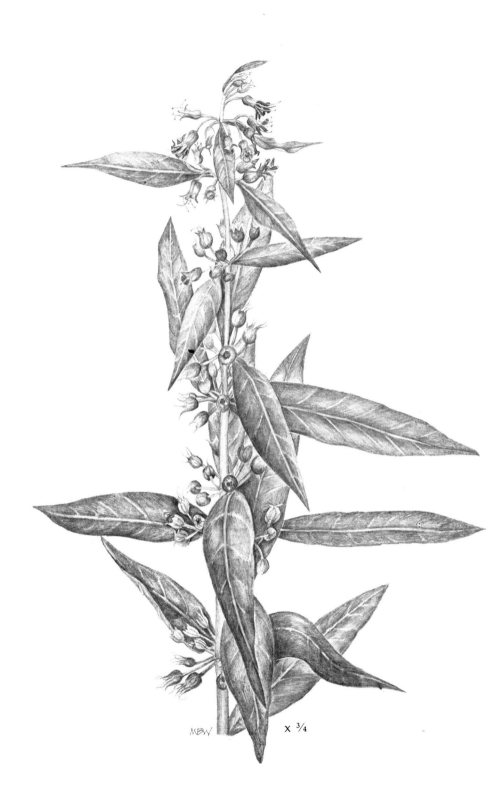

MBW   X ³/₄

Water Willow
Swamp Loosestrife
Decodon verticillatus (L.) Ell. var. *verticillatus*

This shrub-like herb commonly forms thickets in the standing water of marshes or swamps or in tidal freshwater wetlands. Water Willow has opposite or whorled lance-shaped leaves with soft pink flowers projecting from the leaf axils. The stem as it grows characteristically forms an arch, which in many cases allows the tip of the branch to become submerged, where it often roots. This unique feature makes thickets of *Decodon* easily recognizable.

Water Willow is not one of the true willows (*Salix*), which also grow in wetland habitats. True willows are woody shrubs or trees, usually having narrower, alternate leaves, but which do not produce pink flowers. *Decodon* should also not be confused with another plant, *Justicia americana*, also known as Water Willow. *Justicia americana* is an erect herb with white or light purple flowers; it typically occupies sandy or rocky shorelines along streams and rivers. The typical variety of Water Willow ranges along the Atlantic and Gulf coasts and up the Mississippi River Valley.

Water Willow flowers in July and August. Its stems may be over 7 feet long late in the season, August through September, when the plant is in fruit. Though it propagates by seeds, it is also a perennial. Stems each year come up from a submerged woody base, not a true rhizome.

x ³⁄₄

Giant Bulrush
Soft-stem Bulrush
Scirpus validus Vahl.

A majestic rush-like sedge, Giant Bulrush forms colonies in freshwater marshes and may grow to heights of 10 feet. The long round tapering stems are soft to the touch, hence the name Soft-stem Bulrush. The leaves are reduced to inconspicuous sheaths at the base of the stem. The terminal, brownish panicle is evident in mid-summer. Colonies are found in the lower parts of the marsh, often associated with Arrow Arum and Pickerelweed. The stems and underground rhizomes are a favorite food of muskrats. The seeds are eaten by birds. This plant reproduces by both seed and rhizome.

Giant Bulrush can be found in wetland areas throughout most of the continental United States. It is common along the Mid-Atlantic Coast.

X ¾

Soft Rush

Juncus effusus L.

Soft Rush is perhaps the most common rush in coastal freshwater wetlands. It resembles Black Needlerush (*Juncus roemerianus*) of saline marshes, but it is not nearly as stiff nor does it have the very sharp tip of its halophytic relative. It stands 1-1/2 to 3 feet tall. Like its counterpart, however, the branched inflorescence appears to emerge laterally from the stem or culm. The individual yellow-green flowers are minute; the seeds are almost microscopic.

What appears to be the stem is actually a sheath that is part of a leaf that surrounds the stem. The sheath becomes a blade at the point where the inflorescence emerges. The stem has minute ridges or striations visible with a hand lens.

Soft Rush is distributed along the coast from Newfoundland to Texas and throughout much of North America. It is often found in dense clusters or tussocks. It flowers from June through August (as illustrated) and propagates by both seed and rhizome.

Polygonum punctatum Ell.

x ³⁄₄

Smartweeds

Polygonum punctatum Ell.
Polygonum densiflorum Meissner
Polygonum hydropiperoides Michaux

Three species of Smartweeds are commonly found in tidal freshwater marshes along the Mid-Atlantic Coast, *Polygonum punctatum* being the most abundant. These plants are usually associated with Arrow Arum and Pickerelweed in the intertidal zone. The tiny white, green, or pink flowers form a terminal, elongated cluster that blooms from early summer to frost, as illustrated. The stems are round in cross section. The narrow, willow-like leaves, the swollen leaf nodes, and the tissue-like sheath (ocreae) surrounding the leaf node (see Water Dock) are distinguishing features of Smartweeds. Characteristically, the leaves wither and die but remain on the stem until late in the season. The drooping stems are 2 to 3 feet long.

The lustrous black or brown seeds are relished by ducks in the fall. Smartweeds are planted in marshes by both seed and rhizome to attract waterfowl.

P. densiflorum is mainly an Atlantic Coastal Plain plant, whereas the other two species range throughout much of the North American continent.

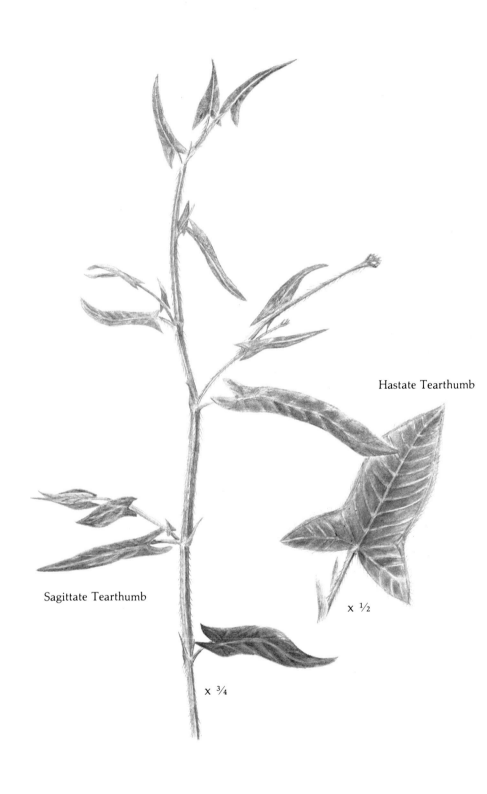

Hastate Tearthumb

Sagittate Tearthumb

x ½

x ¾

Tearthumbs
Sagittate Tearthumb
Polygonum sagittatum L.
Hastate Tearthumb
Polygonum arifolium L.

Tearthumbs are commonly found in freshwater marshes where they form matted intertwining thickets with other marsh plants. Both Sagittate and Hastate Tearthumbs have downward-trending barbs, sharp and strong enough to tear flesh, on their sharply angled stems and leaf petioles, hence the name Tearthumb. The black or dark brown seeds are similar to those of Smartweeds and are eaten by waterfowl.

Although the barbed, sprawling, vine-like stems, 5 to 10 feet long, are common to both species, there are characteristics that distinguish one from the other. Sagittate Tearthumb has narrow, smooth leaves with sagittate basal leaf lobes (pointing downward), whereas Hastate Tearthumb has broad pubescent (downy) leaves with hastate basal lobes(nearly at right angles). These features are indicated in the illustration, which depicts these plants in flower. The flowers are greenish-white.

Both species range throughout the eastern half of the United States and Canada, though Hastate Tearthumb is more prevalent in the coastal areas, especially in the southern part of the Mid-Atlantic region. The Tearthumbs are annuals and propagate by seeds.

x ½

Water Dock
Swamp Dock
Rumex verticillatus L.

Water Dock, an erect, 3- to 4-foot-tall, robust plant with dark green, lance-shaped leaves, grows in dense colonies in tidal freshwater wetlands. The elongated, green flower head (raceme) is evident in late spring or early summer. The flowers (pictured) are yellow-green. By mid-summer to late summer, the flowers are transformed into dry, rusty brown fruits arranged in whorls on the terminal stem. Water Dock propagates by both seed and rhizomes. A thin, tissue-like sheath (ocrea) is located at each leaf node, a distinguishing feature of the family Polygonaceae. The lower leaves wither during the late summer months but remain on the stem until late fall when eventually the entire plant decays. Water Dock seeds are eaten by waterfowl during fall migration.

Water Dock appears to be particularly adapted to tidal freshwater marshes of the Mid-Atlantic Coast, although it is also found in the interior.

X ¼

Marsh Hibiscus
Swamp Cotton
Rose Mallow
Hibiscus moscheutos L.

A tall (3 to 7 feet), leafy perennial, Marsh Hibiscus is commonly found in freshwater marshes or along the upland margin of saline marshes where freshwater seepage dilutes saltier water from the estuary. The large, showy, white or pink blossoms, often 6 inches or more wide, and the rose-red centers of these flowers are distinctive characteristics of this robust plant. It flowers (as illustrated) from late July through August. In the background is a stem from the previous year showing the fruiting heads. The plant propagates by both seeds and rhizomes.

Marsh Hibiscus leaves are alternate, have irregularly serrated edges, and are smooth above and velvety underneath. They are 4 to 6 inches long and 2 to 3 inches wide.

Belonging to the same family (Malvaceae) as cotton, Marsh Hibiscus resembles a cotton plant in bloom and is sometimes called Swamp Cotton. However, it does not develop a cotton ball as does its domesticated relative.

Two other species of this same family grow in tidal marshes in the Mid-Atlantic region. *Althaea officinalis*, the true Marsh Mallow, is rare or infrequent along this part of the coast. During colonial times a confection was made from the mucilaginous roots of this plant, hence the marshmallow of today. A similar plant, *Kosteletzkya virginica*, also called Marsh Mallow, is commonly found in brackish marshes along the Mid-Atlantic Coast. See the text under Marsh Mallow for the distinguishing features of these Mallows.

Marsh Hibiscus is found along the coast from Maryland to Texas.

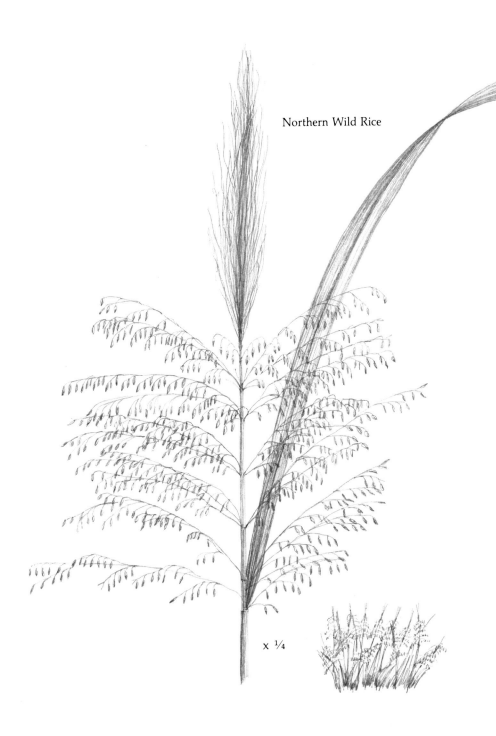

Northern Wild Rice

X ¼

Wild Rice
Northern Wild Rice
Zizania aquatica L.
Southern Wild Rice
Zizaniopsis miliacea (Michaux) Doell & Ascherson

There are two different species of Wild Rice found in the freshwater marshes in this region: Northern Wild Rice and Southern Wild Rice.

Northern Wild Rice (*Zizania aquatica*) is found throughout the region, though in many areas only sparingly. It is found in nontidal as well as tidal freshwater marshes, and it ranges from Maine to Florida along the coast and interior to Minnesota and North Dakota. Its rice-like grains of late fall are highly valued as waterfowl food. However, the soft immature grains of late summer or early autumn are usually eaten by redwinged blackbirds before the great flocks of ducks and geese arrive from the north.

Southern Wild Rice (*Zizaniopsis miliacea*) ranges from Maryland south to Florida and Texas. The leaves of Southern Wild Rice are similar to Northern Wild Rice. However, the panicle of the former species is not separated into distinct reproductive branches. Both pistillate and staminate flowers (spikelets) are on the same branches. The grains of Southern Wild Rice are small and not fit for human consumption; they are, however, eaten by birds.

Wild Rice has different varieties and growth forms. However, the distinguishing characteristic common to all varieties of Northern Wild Rice is the arrangement of the staminate (male) and pistillate (female) flowers on the panicle (inflorescence). The lower branches of the panicle contain the staminate flowers, while the upper part is composed entirely of pistillate flowers that eventually develop into rice grains. (See illustration.) The typical variety of Wild Rice has leaves up to 3 feet long and 2 inches wide. The tiny saw-like teeth on the leaf margins can cut tender skin. The grains of this majestic grass are prized as a gourmet food.

x ¾

Rice Cutgrass
Leersia oryzoides (L.) Swartz

Rice Cutgrass colonies form dense matted, tangled thickets in freshwater marshes and swamps. The grass may obtain heights of 3 feet or more but the stems (culms) become weakened shortly after maturity. During the flowering season, late August to early October, the flowering heads (panicles) are a noticeable yellow-green. They make a definite contrast with the other marsh vegetation, which for the most part is well past the blooming period. The marshes at this point are still green, but most plants are in fruit and some are starting to deteriorate. Rice Cutgrass propagates vegetatively by rhizomes and also by seeds. The flowering stage is illustrated.

The leaf margins of Rice Cutgrass are rough and can easily tear flesh and clothing. They have many minute teeth, hence the name Cutgrass. The dark red grain is eaten by migrating waterfowl and resident marsh birds. Rice Cutgrass is common throughout much of the continental United States in wetland areas such as those along the Mid-Atlantic Coast.

X ²/₃

Walter's Millet
Echinochloa walteri (Pursh) Nash.

Walter's Millet is a robust grass – it grows as tall as 7 feet – frequently found in tidal freshwater marshes, in swales, and in ditches. It has a dense reddish-brown to purple flowering cluster that has a bristly appearance. Each floret (flower) sports a stout, elongated appendage called an awn. Collectively the florets are nearly concealed in this mass of awns, as depicted. The plant flowers in July. When in seed, the cluster (panicle) is often so burdened by its own weight that it nearly touches the ground. Walter's Millet is an annual and propates only via seeds.

The seeds of this wild millet are a highly valued waterfowl food. It is often planted in wetland wildlife refuges to attract migrating waterfowl and to maintain resident populations of marsh birds and shorebirds. Muskrats use the stems and leaves for food and lodge construction.

Walter's Millet is not harvested for human consumption as are other millets in other countries.

Walter's Millet is found along the Atlantic and Gulf coasts from New England to Texas.

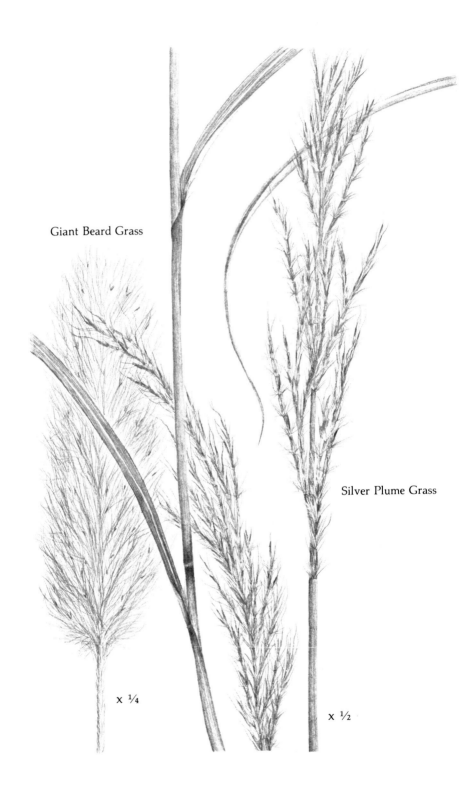

Giant Beard Grass

Silver Plume Grass

x ¼

x ½

Silver Plume Grass
Erianthus brevibarbis Michaux
Giant Beard Grass
Erianthus giganteus (Walter) Muhl.

These two attractive grasses, Silver Plume and Giant Beard, are frequently encountered in the fall in various wetland habitats along the coastal plain from New Jersey to the Gulf Coast. They grow in groups or colonies. Giant Beard Grass (*Erianthus giganteus*), the taller of the two, standing from 12 to 14 feet high, has a feathery fruiting head that can be up to 6 inches broad. Silver Plume Grass, at 8 to 10 feet, is not quite as tall and has a more sparse, narrow head. The flowering head (panicle) of both species has a silvery glint, especially on a sunny day. The stem (culm) and head of both species are often purplish in color. Both species are esthetically pleasing, but they have little wildlife value except for cover. Although Silver Plume Grass and Giant Beard Grass can be found west of the Appalachians, their predominant range is coastal.

In the illustration, Silver Plume Grass (*E. brevibarbis*) is in the foreground, and Giant Beard Grass (*E. giganteus*) is in the background. Both are in fruit. They propagate by both seeds and rhizomes.

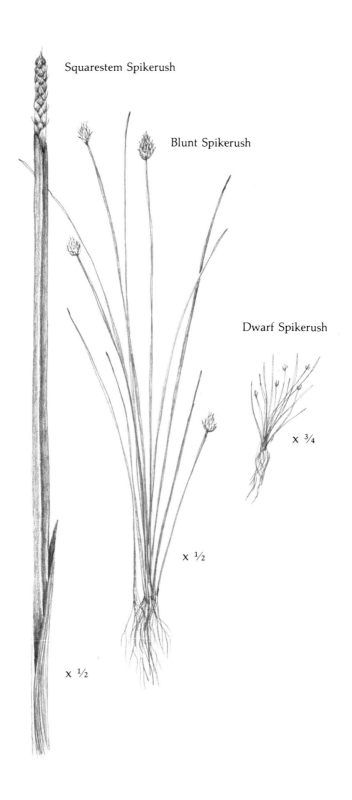

Squarestem Spikerush

Blunt Spikerush

Dwarf Spikerush

x ¾

x ½

x ½

Spikerushes
Squarestem Spikerush
Eleocharis quadrangulata (Michaux) R. & S.
Dwarf Spikerush
Eleocharis parvula (R. & S.) Link.
Blunt Spikerush
Eleocharis obtusa (Willd.) Schultes

The Spikerushes are not true rushes but belong instead to the sedge family (Cyperaceae). Spikerushes are leafless with a terminal flowering or fruiting head. Though there are a number of different species of Spikerushes found in the wetlands of the Mid-Atlantic Coast, the three species illustrated and described here are typical. They are restricted to freshwater marshes except for the Dwarf Spikerush, an occasional plant in brackish marshes.

Squarestem Spikerush is the largest of the Spikerushes. The stem is usually quadrangular or triangular in cross section and will obtain a height of 4 or 5 feet. The spike is cylindrical and elongated.

Dwarf Spikerush is the smallest, rarely standing over 2 inches high. This wiry plant is only occasionally found in brackish marshes, where it is quite inconspicuous.

Blunt Spikerush is a rather stiff medium-sized sedge, ranging from 6 inches to 2 feet tall, capped with a terminal, light brown, cone-like seed head. This species is often found in freshwater marshes.

The seeds and stems of most Spikerushes are eaten by waterfowl and muskrats.

x ½

Royal Fern
Osmunda regalis L. var. *spectabilis* (Willd.) Gray

Royal Fern is one of the most common ferns in tidal freshwater marshes, in swamps, and in swales among coastal dunes. It is tall, its fronds often obtaining a height of 5 feet or more. Royal Fern has spore-forming leaflets (pinnae) at its apex. Its stout rhizomes are covered with persistent frond (leaf) stalks from previous years. The rhizomes of this fern may be over 100 feet long and centuries old. Through the centuries soil accumulates, leaving the older part of the rhizome buried. The youngest part is above ground. Royal Fern also reproduces by spores.

Royal Fern can tolerate occasional salt spray but not salt water on a daily basis. It is likely to be found in the higher, hummocky areas in freshwater marshes and is often associated with the shrubs Button Bush, Swamp Rose, and Silky Dogwood. In fact, a large cluster of Royal Fern fronds looks shrubby and can, at first glance, be mistaken for a woody plant. The young fiddle heads that develop in springtime make excellent eating. In the wild they can be found near the frond stalks from the previous year.

Other ferns — such as Sensitive Fern, Netted Chain Fern, Virginia Chain Fern, and Marsh Fern — are likely to be found in freshwater marshes. These ferns have no stems. Their fronds appear featherlike, and leaflets (pinnae) appear at right angles to the frond stalk (rachis).

Royal Fern is found in Atlantic coast marshes and in wetland habitats throughout much of the East and Midwest.

x ½

Marsh Fern
Thelypteris palustris Schott

Marsh Fern is one of the most common ferns in nonsaline wetland areas along the coast. One can expect to find it in tidal freshwater marshes and swamps, dune field swales, bogs, and pocosins. It stands 1 to 2-1/2 feet tall. The fronds (leaves) originate from slender, creeping rhizomes and are classically pinnately compound, that is, the leaflets (pinnae) are arranged at right angles to the central axis (rachis). Spores are produced in distinct units (sori) on the undersides of the pinnae.) The sori are so dense that almost the entire ventral leaf surface appears dark brown. This stage of the reproductive cycle is most obvious late in the growing season. In certain wetlands, Marsh Fern colonies can successfully outcompete other wetland plants. The young spring fronds, fiddleheads, are quite a delicacy for wild food lovers. These tender coils can be eaten raw in a salad or can be prepared by steaming.

Marsh Fern can be found in wetland habitats throughout much of eastern North America including the Atlantic Seaboard.

x ¾

Beggar's Ticks
Tickseed Sunflower
Bidens coronata (L.) Britt.

In late summer or early fall, many freshwater tidal marshes are aglow with the brilliant yellow sunflower-like blooms of Beggar's Ticks, which stand 2 to 4 feet tall. Throughout the spring and most of the summer months, however, these plants are inconspicuous among other dense vegetation. They are single-stemmed or sparingly branched. The characteristic twin-bristled fruit of Beggar's Ticks or "stick tight" is familiar to most who venture into wet places in the fall and later find the fruits attached to their clothing.

The species of *Bidens* featured here is but one of several found in coastal freshwater wetlands. Of the others, *Bidens laevis* is the most common in these habitats and is predominantly a coastal species. The main difference between the two are leaf characteristics. *Bidens leavis* has simple opposite leaves, whereas *Bidens coronata* has opposite, compound, or divided leaves.

Another yellow-blooming herb found in freshwater marshes, the robust Sneezeweed (*Helenium autumnale*), can be confused with Beggar's Ticks.

Bidens laevis is predominantly a coastal plant and ranges from New England to the Gulf Coast. *Bidens coronata* is a more northern herb, ranging from the Maritimes to North Carolina as well as westward to Nebraska.

X ½

Sneezeweed
Wingstem
Helenium autumnale L.

The tall perennial called Sneezeweed is aptly named, for its pollen can provoke violent sneezing. Nonetheless, it is an attractive, multi-branched, robust plant with many bright-yellow flowering heads. It may grow over 6 feet tall. Sneezeweed is found in wet pastures, in low meadows, and frequently in tidal freshwater marshes. It should be distinguished from Beggar's Ticks (*Bidens coronata*), a similar-looking yellow-blooming herb that grows in the same habitat. Both plants have yellow heads but those of *Helenium* have more globular tan or beige centers. *Helenium* has alternate leaves whereas *Bidens* has opposite leaves. *Helenium* is also known as Wingstem because of the continuous, long, narrow, wafer-like appendages that extend in a parallel mode on the stem. It propagates by seeds.

Sneezeweed can be found in tidal marshes throughout the Mid-Atlantic Coast. The flowering stage is illustrated.

x ¼

Reed Grass
Phragmites
Phragmites australis (Cav.) Trin. ex. Steud.

A tall coarse grass with a feathery seed head, Reed Grass is a familiar invader of disturbed low or marshy areas. The broad, acutely tapering leaves, the characteristic seed head, and the very long rhizomes are the trademarks of this giant grass that grows to 12 feet high.

Reed Grass becomes established via seeds but spreads mainly by rhizomes. The long (up to 20 feet or more), creeping rhizomes of this aggressive plant enable it to vegetatively propagate dredged spoil areas quickly, a valued attribute in controlling erosion of dredged spoil deposition areas. However, in some freshwater marshes Reed Grass often outcompetes other more valuable marsh plants such as Wild Rice and Big Cordgrass. This competition is of potential concern to wetland managers.

Reed Grass is a cosmopolitan plant found throughout the world in both tidal and nontidal freshwater marshes. In Eastern Europe fibers from its tough, thick stems are used for making paper. Though considered a valuable plant in its natural habitats in Europe where it is kept in check by natural biological controls, Reed Grass is considered a weedy invader by most marsh managers on this side of the Atlantic.

The feathery inflorescence of Phragmites is dark brown when in flower and fades to tan when the fruits (seeds) develop. The fruits are tiny (1/16 of an inch). The length of the inflorescence varies from 6 to 12 inches long and 3 to 6 inches wide.

Reed Grass is found mainly in areas that have been disturbed throughout the Mid-Atlantic Coast. The plant is drawn as it would look from July through September.

X ³/₄

Swamp Milkweed
Ascelpias incarnata L. var. *pulchra* (Willd.) Woodson

The tall, leafy, pink-flowered herb called Swamp Milkweed is commonly found in tidal freshwater marshes but is seldom a dominant component of this richly diverse wetland. In mid-summer, Swamp Milkweed produces a large number of unusual flowers. As is true of milkweeds in general, each flower has a specialized morphology so unique that cross-pollination, typically via butterflies, is quite complicated. The pollen is concentrated into minute waxy masses called pollinia (resembling two sacks attached to each other by a filament called a translator). Each pollinium is carried from one flower (via the tiny spurs of the butterfly's leg) to another flower where it must be precisely inserted to insure pollination. The reproductive mechanism is apparently not always fulfilled since milkweed plants produce few fruits late in the season.

The fruits that do develop are robust pods, botanically known as follicles. Inside the follicles are many seeds with long silky hairs resembling kapok. When the seeds are released they are widely distributed by the wind.

Both flower and fruit stages are drawn. The seed pod is in the lower-left-hand corner on a separate plant.

Swamp Milkweed leaves are opposite, lance-shaped, and have smooth margins. The leaves sport dense, minute hairs that make them velvety to the touch. The stems are 2 to 4 feet tall. The plant reproduces via seeds and vegetatively via rhizomes.

This variety of Swamp Milkweed is found in wetlands along the Atlantic Seaboard from Canada to Florida.

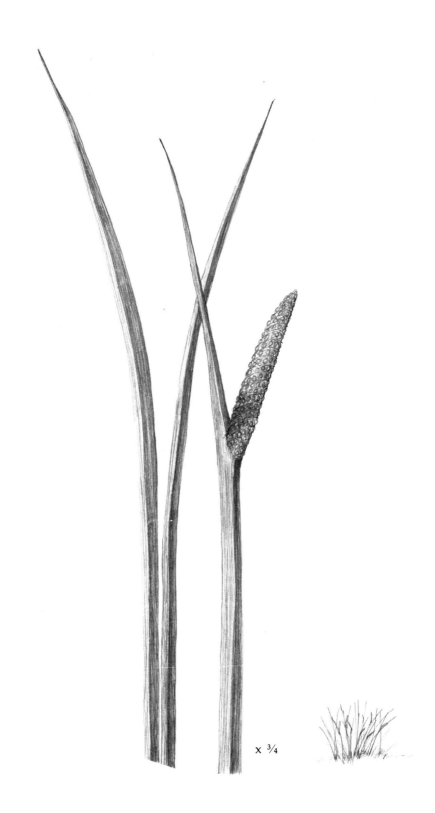

X ¾

Sweet Flag
Acorus calamus L.

Sweet Flag grows 2 to 5 feet tall in dense colonies in freshwater marshes. It propagates mainly by rhizomes. The general appearance of Sweet Flag is similar to that of grasses or sedges with wide sword-like leaf blades. Upon closer observation, however, it can be seen that elongated, cylindrical inflorescences emerge from the leaf-like stems. This reproductive appendage is called a spadix, a spike of compacted fleshy flowers. This structure is similar to that of Arrow Arum, except in Sweet Flag the spadix is not surrounded by a spathe, the spathe here appearing as a continuation of the stem.

Sweet Flag is so named because all parts of the plant, particularly the rhizomes, have a sweet aromatic taste and odor. During early colonial settlement, the foliage of *Acorus* was cut and strewn upon the floors of the colonists' primitive dwellings. When tread upon repeatedly, the material emitted a sweet fragrance, hence the earliest household air freshener.

Though Sweet Flag is apparently eaten as a natural food, I don't recommend it on grounds of taste. The roots and rhizomes are also a favorite food of muskrats.

Acorus is found throughout the Atlantic Seaboard as well as throughout the continental United States. The plant is depicted as it would appear June through July.

X ¾

Jewelweed
Touch-me-not
Clearweed
Impatiens capensis Meerb.

Jewelweed is often found in coastal freshwater marshes, especially where there is shade from trees along the upland margins. It is a delightful plant with pale green, translucent stems and curiously shaped, orange-yellow flowers (1 to 1-1/2 inches long) with brown spots. The flower is not unlike a miniature cornucopia. The leaves are alternately arranged and are thin but succulent; they contain a large volume of sap. Jewelweed is also called Touch-me-not because the seeds suddenly burst from the capsule when pressure is applied. Its leaves are alternate, simple, and very soft. They are green on the upper side and pale or slightly gray underneath. The plant stands 1-1/2 to 3 feet tall. It is an annual and propagates only by seeds.

The juice from this plant has been reported to counteract the toxin of Poison Ivy (*Rhus radicans*). The juice is extracted by crushing the stems, and the crushed mass is applied to the afflicted part of the body before any visible reaction to the toxin has occurred. After a rash and/or blisters appear, it apparently has no effect. Experts and naturalists disagree as to whether or not this works.

Jewelweed is widely distributed throughout much of eastern North America. It ranges throughout the Mid-Atlantic Coast.

x 1

Asian Spiderwort
Aneilema keisak Hassk.

Aneilema keisak is a succulent flowering herb with grass-like foliage. The plant is often abundant, forming dense mats in tidal freshwater marshes and swamps and other wetlands such as ponds and ditches. Asian Spiderwort was apparently introduced into the Mid-Atlantic region early in the twentieth century and has spread rapidly in the southeast. In some open swamps it outcompetes native species and totally dominates the ground cover through its aggressive nature and its ability to tolerate shade.

Each stem of Asian Spiderwort may have several small (3/8 of an inch wide) pink flowers with three distinct petals. The flowers are found terminally and along the stem. *Aneilema* is closely related to the Spiderworts and Dayflowers and is occasionally associated with Virginia Dayflower in swamps. The flowering stage is illustrated. The plant stands 6 inches to 2 feet tall. Its unbranched stems sport pale green leaves 1 to 3 inches long. It is an annual and propagates via seeds.

Asian Spiderwort is found in wetlands from coastal Virginia to Georgia.

x ¾

Ironweed

Vernonia noveboracensis (L.) Michaux

Ironweed is a 4- to 7-foot-tall, leafy perennial with many royal purple flowering heads. It is commonly found in open wetlands and is frequently found above mean high water in tidal freshwater marshes. Its blooms resemble thistle heads, not surprising since they both belong to the Compositae family. Unlike thistles, however, the Ironweed plant is not spiny. Each flower head (composite) is composed of 30 to 50 tiny individual flowers, an identifying characteristic of this family. The flowering stage is illustrated.

Ironweed is a multibranched plant. Its leaves are alternate and have serrated margins. They are smooth on their upper sides and have dense velvety hairs on their undersides. The plant propagates by seeds but is also a perennial, its stems originating year after year from an underground structure called a crown (something like a bulb but amorphic and difficult to describe).

Ironweed usually grows in the richly diverse higher freshwater marsh zone and is usually associated with a number of other marsh species such as Marsh Hibiscus, Swamp Milkweed, Big Cordgrass, and Royal Fern.

As with many common names, the meaning/origins of the name Ironweed have been lost through history. Most common names used in North America had their beginnings during the Middle Ages. Many plants in the New World resemble plants in Europe. When Europeans first arrived they applied these old names to similar plants found here. It is my understanding (though the information is not documented and is purely speculative) that a similar plant in Europe is called Ironweed because it grows in bogs where bog iron was mined in the fifteenth century.

Ironweed is mainly a coastal herb, ranging from New England to the Gulf of Mexico.

x ¼

Saw Grass
Cladium jamaicense Crantz

Saw Grass is not a grass at all. It belongs to the Cyperaceae or sedge family. It is a southern species that ranges along the coast from extreme southeastern Virginia to Texas on the Gulf Coast. Saw Grass reaches its greatest abundance in the Florida Everglades. While it can reproduce by seeds, Saw Grass progagates mainly vegetatively by rhizomes. The fruiting stage is depicted.

Cladium jamaicense is a 5- to 10-foot-tall, coarse sedge with triangular culms and long, narrow stem leaves. The leaf margins have minute sawtooth-like bristles that can be devastating to unprotected flesh. From summer through autumn, this sedge is easily recognized by a series of globose, dark brown fruits or light green flower clusters. Saw Grass is often abundant and forms extensive, dense stands in coastal freshwater or low saline wetlands. In brackish marshes it is usually found near the upland margin where salinity is reduced by upland seepage and runoff.

X ¾

Water Hemlock
Beaver Poison
Cicuta maculata L.

Water Hemlock is a leafy, branching, 3- to 6-foot-tall herb with pinnately compound leaves. The leaves are divided into leaflets arranged along a central axis. The leaves immediately subtending the flower head are usually divided into 3 parts. Farther down the stem the compound leaves may be divided into 15 or more leaflets.

In summer, the plant produces an unusual, radially branched inflorescence (umbel) with a multitude of tiny white flowers. The head gently resembles that of Queen Anne's Lace or Wild Carrot. The swollen, tuber-like roots and stems of this plant are extremely poisonous. The lower part of the stem is hollow, and there are records of children making and using whistles or peashooters from this part of the plant, inadvertently poisoning themselves.

A closely related Eurasian plant, Poison Hemlock (*Conium maculatum*), which has since been introduced to the New World, was very likely the cause of Socrates' death.

Water Hemlock is often found in freshwater wetland areas throughout much of North America as well as throughout the Mid-Atlantic coastal region. It grows in various wetland habitats such as ditches, swales, and the edges of swamps. The flowering stage is illustrated.

x 1

Climbing Hempweed
Mikania scandens (L.) Willd.

Among the dense and diverse vegetation of a tidal freshwater marsh, this twining perennial often forms a matted tangle that makes walking through such areas a difficult task. Climbing Hempweed is one of the few members of the Compositae family that is a vine.

Mikania has opposite heart-shaped leaves and fairly dense flower clusters. Each individual head in the cluster is made up of four tiny flowers. The clusters vary from white to pink in color. The foliage of this vine could be mistaken for Morning Glory, but the flowers are totally different and one could not confuse the two. The flowering stage is illustrated. Climbing Hempweed propagates by both seed and rhizome.

Though climbing Hempweed is mainly a coastal species, it can occasionally be found as far west as Missouri. Although it ranges as far north as Maine, it is much more common in tropical South America. It is found throughout the Mid-Atlantic coastal region.

Carex vulpinoidea Michaux

Carex lurida Wahlenberg

x ³⁄₄

x ³⁄₄

Sedges
Carex vulpinoidea Michaux
Carex lurida Wahlenberg

The word sedge generally refers to any plant that is a member of the sedge family, Cyperaceae. Most of the many sedges belonging to the genus *Carex* do not have specific common names, primarily because many of them look so much alike that identification is difficult. The two species presented here are commonly found in coastal wetland habitats. They stand 1 to 2 feet tall.

Species belonging to this genus have one common characteristic: their nutlike fruit is surrounded by a minute, parchment-like sac called a perigynium. In *Carex lurida*, the perigynium has a needle-like appendage as seen in the illustration. These fruiting structures are compacted into distinct fruiting heads situated terminally on the stem.

Carex vulpinoidea has a chaff-like perigynium. Its fruiting structures are compacted into clusters at the tip of the stem. Both species reproduce by both seed and rhizome.

The leaves of these sedges are long, narrow, and grass-like. The stems are triangular in cross section and usually pea green in color. Their minute flowers are compacted into light green heads, which when fruiting turn tan. The fruiting stage is illustrated.

Sedges dominate in certain wetland areas such as sedge meadows and sedge bogs. They are also found in dune swales, tidal freshwater swamps, marshes, and other wet habitats. The two sedges featured here are not, however, halophytic. Sedges grow in widely varying habitats—some in standing water, some where the soil only needs to be moist, still others in dry conditions.

Waterfowl and rodents eat the seeds of these plants and utilize the plants themselves for cover and nesting areas.

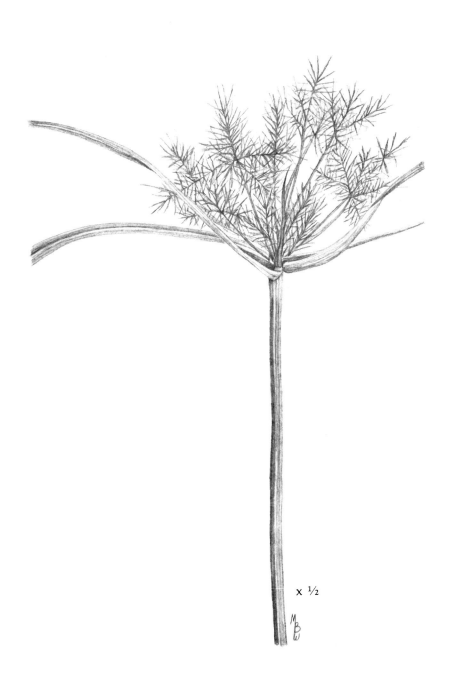

x ½

M
B
W

Chufa
Galingale, Nut Grass
Cyperus esculentus L.

Chufa is a very common sedge of wetlands throughout the world. It is often considered a weed in cultivated fields, particularly if the fields have been reclaimed from wetlands. There are a number of species within this genus that are common to wetland habitats, but Chufa is perhaps the most well known. Its underground, nut-like tubers are considered a delicacy and have been known as such since the time of the pharaohs. The tubers can be eaten raw or lightly cooked and seasoned. They are also relished by waterfowl. Chufa reproduces by both seeds and tubers.

A mature plant, which stands 1 to 3 feet tall, has a dense umbrella-shaped complex of flowering rays. Each ray supports a spike of flowers that resembles a bottle brush. This entire reproductive structure is yellow-brown in color.

The flowering stem (culm) is stout and triangular-shaped, and leaves (bracts) immediately subtend the inflorescence. Grass-like basal leaves are also present.

Chufa ranges throughout the Mid-Atlantic coastal region in freshwater marshes. Depicted is the plant as it would appear July through September.

x ½

False Nettle
Boehmeria cylindrica (L.) Sw.

False Nettle is an erect perennial that superficially looks like a mint. The two, however, are not even closely related. False Nettle does have opposite leaves and squarish stems, typical mint characteristics. However, the floral structure of mints is more elaborate. False Nettle resembles Stinging Nettle (*Urtica*) to which it is closely related, though fortunately it does not have those nasty stinging hairs. The small green flowers (lacking petals and sepals) are borne on densely crowded spikes originating at the axil of the leaf petioles. False Nettle grows along the upland/freshwater marsh border and in swales in coastal dune fields. It is found in these habitats along the Mid-Atlantic Coast and is also widely distributed in wetland areas throughout much of the eastern United States.

False Nettle stands 2 to 5 feet tall, usually grows in colonies, and propagates by both seed and rhizome. The flowering stage is drawn.

X ³⁄₄

Sweetpepper Bush
White Alder
Clethra alnifolia L.

Sweetpepper Bush is a coastal freshwater wetland shrub commonly found along the Atlantic and Gulf coasts from Maine to Texas. It has simple alternate leaves that resemble elm leaves. In mid-summer, the shrub produces a terminal inflorescence (raceme) of small white flowers.

Although Sweetpepper Bush is typically found along the banks of tidal waterways in coastal swamps, it often grows in maritime bogs and pocosins, particularly in the southern part of the Mid-Atlantic region. It is frequently associated with other shrubs such as Swamp Rose, Button Bush, and Alder. This species could possibly be confused with Alder because the leaves are similar, but true Alders do not produce white flowers and their fruits are cone-like.

Sweetpepper Bush grows up to 12 feet tall and propagates by seeds. Its gray fruits somewhat resemble peppercorns — perhaps the origin of the common name.

x ½

Button Bush

Cephalanthus occidentalis L.

Button Bush is commonly found along the upland margins or on raised hummocks in freshwater marshes. It stands 4 to 10 feet tall. Its stems are multibranched. The leaves are leathery smooth on the upper surface and have even margins. They are oppositely arranged or whorled with 3 or more leaves emerging from one point on the stem. A distinguishing feature is the leaf petioles, often reddish in color.

From early summer through late fall, a striking, white, ball-like inflorescence emerges (as drawn). Delicate elongate stigmas that extend from each tubular flower give the flower cluster the appearance of a globular pincushion. The resulting fruits (nutlets) are compacted into a brown sphere, a distinguishing feature during late fall and early winter. The seeds are eaten by Wood Ducks.

Button Bush is often associated with other freshwater wetland shrubs such as Sweetpepper Bush, Swamp Rose, and Swamp Dogwood. This shrub is widely distributed throughout much of the United States and throughout the Mid-Atlantic Coast as well.

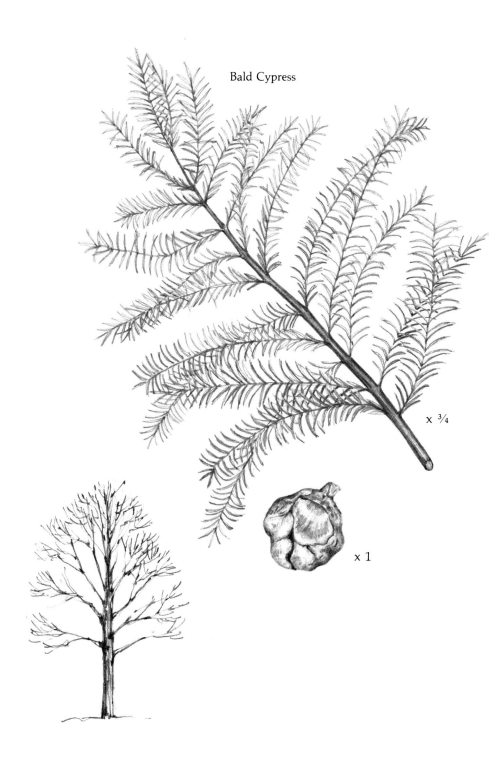

Bald Cypress

x ¾

x 1

Bald Cypress
Taxodium distichum (L.) Richard
Pond Cypress
Taxodium ascendens Brongn.

Bald Cypress is perhaps the most majestic swamp species in the south, reaching heights up to 120 feet. In the Mid-Atlantic region, this tree often dominates tidal and nontidal coastal wetlands. Bald Cypress is an exception among conifers in that it is deciduous. Its needles turn a rusty brown in the fall and are entirely gone by winter, hence the name Bald Cypress. The female cones are woody and nearly spherical, shedding winged seeds in October.

"Cypress knees," a common feature of this species, are actually unbranched shoots originating from the roots. The wood of the knees is lighter and more porous than the wood of the trunk and is thought to aid in oxygen exchange for the submerged roots. The bark is stringy and flakes away from the wood longitudinally.

The wood is highly valued for its resistance to decay. Because of its durability, it is used for making shingles, posts, and railroad ties and in boat construction. Though there are still many mature stands in isolated areas, large tracts of swamps have been logged for Cypress. One giant Cypress with a trunk diameter of 13 feet was recorded in Florida. Trees half this size are known to be nearly 1,000 years old.

Pond Cypress (*Taxodium ascendens*) is also found in coastal swamps and pocosins along the coast from Virginia to Florida. It is similar to Bald Cypress except for its needles, which are scale-like and appressed to the slender branches.

Bald Cypress is a favorite perching site for herons, egrets, and other water birds. Wood Ducks nest in its hollow trunks.

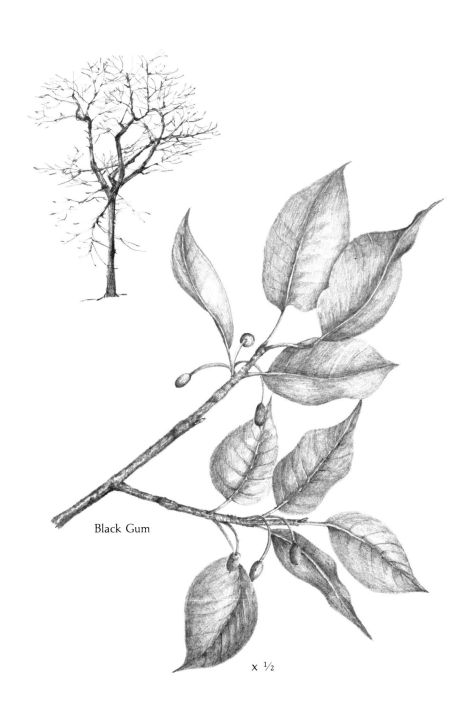

Black Gum

x ½

Black Gum
Nyssa sylvatica Marshall var. *biflora* (Walter) Sargent
Tupelo Gum
Nyssa aquatica L.

The gums are commonly found in coastal freshwater swamps in the Mid-Atlantic region. The smooth, elliptic leaves of Black Gum are alternately arranged and in early autumn change to a brilliant red, usually long before other trees begin to turn. Blue, berry-like fruits (drupes), 1/2 to 3/4 of an inch long, appear in late summer, solitary or in twos or threes. They are eaten by raccoons, opossums, and various species of birds.

Tupelo Gum is similar to Black Gum except for its larger (1 to 1-1/2 inches long) solitary fruits. The leaves of Tupelo Gum may have a few teeth on their margins. Tupelo Gum ranges from southeastern Virginia to Florida along the Atlantic Seaboard. Black Gum has a more extensive distribution and is often found on drier upland areas. In coastal swamps, both species are often associated with Bald Cypress and Red Maple, and both grow to heights of 80 to 100 feet. In the northern part of the region, Black Gum is often found in low depressions or swales in the maritime forest.

These trees are perching sites for egrets and herons. Raccoons and owls live in the hollow trunks and branches.

The wood from Tupelo is light and close grained and is prized in the South by those who carve decoys.

X ³⁄₄

Red Maple
Acer rubrum L.

Red Maple, a medium-sized tree standing 40 to 50 feet tall, is often found in tidal freshwater swamps, in bogs, and on wet bottomlands. Though it grows in upland areas, during periods of drought it is one of the first trees to lose its leaves. In coastal swamps it is often associated with Tupelo Gum and Bald Cypress in the southern part of the Mid-Atlantic region, and with Atlantic White Cedar (*Chamaecyparis thyoides*) and White Swamp Oak (*Quercus bicolor*) in the northern part. Red Maple gets its name from its reddish flowers in the spring, its red-winged seeds, and its shiny red twigs noticeable in winter. This species is widely distributed throughout the eastern United States.

Appendix A

National Seashores and Wildlife Refuges along the Mid-Atlantic Coast

Delaware

Bombay Hook National Wildlife Refuge
R.D. 1, Box 174
Smyrna, Delaware 19977

Prime Hook National Wildlife Refuge
Milton, Delaware 19968

Maryland

Assateague Island National Seashore
P.O. Box 294
Berlin, Maryland 21811

Blackwater National Wildlife Refuge
Route 1, Box 121
Cambridge, Maryland 21613

Eastern Neck National Wildlife Refuge
Route 2, Box 225
Rock Hall, Maryland 21661

New Jersey

Brigantine, Barnegat, Supawna Meadows National Wildlife Refuges
Great Creek Road
Box 72
Oceanville, New Jersey 08231

New York

Fire Island National Seashore
120 Laurel St.
Patchogue, New York 11772

Target Rock, Amagansett, Conscience Point, Morton, Oyster Bay, Seatuck, Wertheim National Wildlife Refuges
RFD #3, Target Rock Rd.
Huntington, New York 11743

North Carolina

Cape Hatteras National Seashore
Route 1, Box 695
Manteo, North Carolina 27964

Cape Lookout National Seashore
P.O. Box 690
Beaufort, North Carolina 28516

Cedar Island and Swanquarter National Wildlife Refuges
Route 1, Box N-2
Swanquarter, North Carolina 27885

Pea Island National Wildlife Refuge
Box 150
Rodanthe, North Carolina 27968

Virginia

Back Bay, Fisherman Island, Plum Tree Island National Wildlife Refuges
Suite 218, 287 Pembroke Office Park
Virginia Beach, Virginia 23462

Chincoteague, Wallops Island National Wildlife Refuges
Box 62
Chincoteague, Virginia 23336

Great Dismal Swamp National Wildlife Refuge
680 B Carolina Road
Suffolk, Virginia 23434

Mason Neck National Wildlife Refuge
9502 Richmond Highway
Suite A
Lorton, Virginia 22079

Presquile National Wildlife Refuge
Box 620
Hopewell, Virginia 23860

Appendix B

Coastal State Parks and Wildlife Areas along the Mid-Atlantic Coast

Delaware

Department of Natural Resources and
Environmental Control
Division of Parks and Recreation
P.O. Box 1401
Dover, Delaware 19901

State Parks

Cape Henlopen
Delaware Seashore
Fort Delaware

Wildlife Areas

Assawoman
Augustine
Little Creek
Woodland Beach

Maryland

Department of Natural Resources
Tawes State Office Building
Annapolis, Maryland 21401

State Parks

Assateague
Calvert Cliffs
Elk Neck
Gunpowder
Janes Island
Point Lookout
Sandy Point

Management Areas

Cedar Island
Deal Island
E. A. Vaughn
Ellis Bay
Fishing Bay
Pocomoke Sound
Taylors Island

New Jersey

Division of Parks & Forestry
P.O. Box 1420
Trenton, New Jersey 08625

State Parks

Cape May Point
Corson's Inlet
Island Beach

Wildlife Management and Natural Areas

Absecon
Dennis Creek
Egg Island
Great Bay Boulevard
Heislerville
Manasquan River
North Brigantine
Port Republic

New York

State Parks & Recreation
Empire State Plaza
Albany, New York 12238

State Parks

Montauk Downs
Montauk Point
Orient Beach
Robert Moses

Wildlife Management Area

Connetquot River

North Carolina

Department of Natural Resources
and Community Development
P.O. Box 27687
Raleigh, North Carolina 27611

State Parks

Fort Macon
Hammoths Beach
Jockeys Ridge
Theodore Roosevelt

Game Lands

North Carolina has an extensive system of wildlife
areas too numerous to mention. Information can be obtained
from:

North Carolina Wildlife Resources Commission
Raleigh, North Carolina 27611

Virginia

Division of State Parks
1201 Washington Building
Capitol Square
Richmond, Virginia 23219

State Parks

Chippokes Plantation
False Cape
Mason Neck
Seashore
Westmoreland
York River

Natural Areas

Charles C. Stierly Heron Rookery
Parkers Marsh
Wreck Island

Glossary

ANTHESIS. Flowering period.

APPRESSED. Pressed against, as in leaves pressed close to the stem of a plant.

AWN. An elongated bristle usually found associated with grass florets.

AXILE (AXILLARY). The interior angle formed by the stem and the petiole. For example, an axillary flower is one inserted between the stem and petiole.

AXIS. The central stem of an inflorescence.

BARRIER BEACH. A long, narrow, sandy spit connected to the mainland that shelters open water and/or marshes behind it.

BARRIER ISLAND. Lying just off the mainland, a long, narrow, sandy island that shelters open water and/or marshes behind it.

BASAL. Arising from the base of the stem.

BLOWOUT. A depression in sand dunes created by wind; usually devoid of vegetation.

BRACT. A leaf from the axil from which a flower or floral axis arises; a leaf borne on a floral axis.

COLONY. A group of plants that originate vegetatively from rootstocks or rhizomes.

COMPOSITE. An organ made up of several to many distinct parts; more specifically referring to the compound flowering head of species of the Compositae family.

CUTICLE. A protective waxy coating found on the epidermis of leaves or stems of certain plants.

CULM. The stem that terminates in an inflorescence, usually pertaining to grasses, sedges, and rushes.

DECIDUOUS. Falling off or shed seasonally or at a certain stage in the life cycle.

DECUMBENT. Reclining on the ground but with ascending apex or extremity.

DETRITUS. Dead vegatative material in various stages of decomposition.

DIOECIOUS. Having staminate (male) and pistillate (female) flowers on different plants.

DRUPE. A fleshy, single-seed fruit such as a peach or a plum.

ELLIPTIC. Shaped like an ellipse, oval. Referring to the shape of leaves.

ECOTONE. A transition zone between two distinct plant communities.

ENDEMIC. An organism limited to a particular region, ecosystem, or habitat.

FLORET. A very small individual flower, especially one of the small flowers forming the head of a composite plant. In grasses the florets lack defined sepals and petals.

FOLLICLE. A dry fruit that opens along one suture, such as that of the milkweed plant.

GLABROUS. Without hairs; smooth.

GRASS. A common name of members of the Grass Family (Poaceae).

HALOPHYTE. A salt-tolerant plant.

HASTATE. Referring to the shape of the basal lobes of a leaf. Triangular with sharply pointed lobes spreading at right angles away from the base of the leaf stalk.

HUMMOCK (ALSO HAMMOCK). A high area in a marsh, usually supporting trees or shrubs or both.

INFLORESCENCE. The part of the plant that bears flowers.

INLET. A connecting waterway between the sea (or large parent body of water) and a bay, a lagoon, or a sound behind a barrier island or beach.

INTERTIDAL. That area of the shoreline or wetland flooded by regular tides, between mean low tide and mean high tide.

INTRODUCED PLANT. A plant not native to the New World, usually introduced by man either purposely or accidentally.

INVOLUCRE. An aggregate of small, leaf-like whorls or bracts that surround a flower cluster.

LATEX. Plant sap that contains natural rubber compounds.

MARSH PEAT. The substrate upon which the marsh plants grow, composed of partially decayed organic matter mixed with sediments. The top eight to ten inches is laced with rhizomes and roots.

MORPHOLOGY. The structure or form of plants or animals.

NICHE (ECOLOGICAL NICHE). A habitat supplying the factors necessary for the functional role of an organism or species within a community or ecosystem.

NODE. A point on a stem at which a leaf or leaves are inserted.

NUTLET. A miniature nut. A small, dry, single-seeded fruit.

OCREA. A sheath or tissue-like appendage surrounding a leaf node.

OVERWASH. A sand flat usually found behind primary dunes, created by storm surges.

PANICLE. A complex, highly branched, elongated inflorescence. The branches themselves are also branched.

PANNES. Depressions in salt marshes that have no tidal communication.

PAPPUS. The bristle-like or plume-like appendages of tiny fruits.

PEDUNCLE. A stalk that supports an inflorescence or flower.

PELTATE. A stalk or leaf petiole that supports the leaf near the central part of the blade.

PERENNIAL. A plant that lives for several years or longer, usually plants having rhizomes.

PETIOLE. The leaf stalk.

PIEDMONT. The hilly or rolling physiographic region between the Appalachians and the coastal plain.

PINNAE. Leaflets of a compound leaf, such as in ferns.

PISTILLATE. Flowers having only pistils (female reproductive organs).

POCOSIN. An upland swamp of the coastal plain of the southeastern United States.

PRIMARY DUNES. A dune system found adjacent to the beach, also known as fore dunes.

PUBESCENT. Covered with fine soft short hairs; downy.

RACEME. An elogated inflorescence in which the secondary branches are not divided.

RHIZOME. An underground stem, usually elongated, horizontal, and producing aerial shoots.

RUSH. A common name applied to the species belonging to the Rush family (Juncaceae).

SAGITTATE. Referring to the shape of the basal lobes of a leaf. Elongated, triangular, and having the two sharply pointed lobes pointing downward.

SALTBUSH. A common name referring to bushes that live in salt or brackish marshes, namely Marsh Elder and Groundsel Tree.

SEDGE. A common name applied to species belonging to the Sedge family (Cyperaceae).

SERRATE. Notched or toothed on the edge.

SHEATH. An elongated cylindrical structure (usually part of a leaf) that surrounds the stem, as in grasses, sedges, or rushes.

SPADIX. A spike of fleshy flowers as found in Arrow Arum and Sweet Flag.

SPIKE. An elongated, unbranched inflorescence. The flowers are usually densely compacted.

SPOIL DEPOSITION AREA. An area where dredged material or spoil is placed.

STAMINATE. Referring to stamens; flowers having stamens only.

STIGMA. That part of the pistil that receives pollen.

SUBTEND. To be situated below, as in a bract inserted beneath a flower.

SUCCULENT PLANT. A plant with fleshy tissues designed to conserve moisture and maintain an effective water balance.

SWALE. A low-lying depression often with wetland vegetation.

TRANSPIRATION. The evaporation of water from the leaves of plants.

TUFT. A dense clump, cluster, or colony of vegetation as found in many grasses, sedges, and rushes.

UMBEL. A flat-topped or slightly rounded inflorescence.

WETLANDS. Land or areas (as tidal flats or swamps) containing much soil moisture.

WRACK LINE. A zone of debris left by storms or spring tides.

Bibliography

Ansell, H. B. 1903–1912. *Recollections*. 1:62–3. Southern Historical Collection, University of North Carolina, Chapel Hill.

Art, H. W., Bormann, F. H. and Woodwell, G. M. 1974. Barrier Island Forest Ecosystem. *Science* 184:60–2.

Au, S. 1970. "Vegetation and Ecological Processes on Shackleford Bank, North Carolina." Ph.D. dissertation, Duke University, Durham, N.C.

Beal, E. O. 1977. *A Manual of Marsh and Aquatic Vascular Plants of North Carolina*. North Carolina Agricultural Experiment Station, Raleigh, N.C.

Boulé, M. E. 1976. "Geomorphic Interpretation of Vegetation on Fisherman Island, Virginia." M.A. thesis. College of William and Mary, Williamsburg, Va.

Bourdeau, P. F., and Oosting, H. J. 1959. The Maritime Live Oak Forest in North Carolina. *Ecology* 40(1):148–52.

Boyce, S. G. 1954. The Salt Spray Community. *Ecological Monographs* 24(1):29–67.

Brown, C. A. 1959. *Botanical Reconnaissance of the Outer Banks of North Carolina*. Baton Rouge: Louisiana State University Press.

Burk, C. 1961. "A Floristic Study of the Outer Banks of North Carolina." Ph.D. dissertation. University of North Carolina, Chapel Hill, N.C.

Chabreck, R. H., and Condrey, R. E. 1979. *Common Vascular Plants of the Louisiana Marsh*. Louisiana State University Center for Wetlands Resources, Baton Rouge, La.

Chambliss, C. E. 1941. The Botany and History of *Zizania aquatica* L. *Ann. Rept. Smithsonian Inst. 1941*:369–82.

Chapman, V. J. 1960. *Salt Marshes and Salt Deserts of the World*. New York: Interscience Publishers.

Chrysler, M. A. 1930. The Origin and Development of the Vegetation of Sandy Hook. *Bulletin of the Torrey Botanical Club* 57:163–78.

Coker, W. C., and Totten, H. R. 1973. *Trees of the Southeastern States*. Chapel Hill: University of North Carolina Press.

Cooper, A. W. 1974. Salt Marshes. In Odum, H. T., Copeland, B. J., and McMahan, E. A., eds., *Coastal Ecological Systems of the United States*. Vol. 2. Conservation Foundation, Washington, D.C.

Dueser, R. D. et al. 1976. The Virginia Coast Reserve Study, Ecosystem Description. The Nature Conservancy, Arlington, Va.

Dunbar, G. S. 1956. *Geographical History of the Carolina Banks*. Coastal Studies Institute Technical Report No. 8. Chapel Hill, N.C.

Duncan, W. H. 1974. Vascular Halophytes of the Atlantic and Gulf Coasts of North America North of Mexico. In Reimold, R. J., and Queen, W. E., eds., *Ecology of Halophytes*. New York: Academic Press.

Duncan, W. H., and Foote, L. E. 1975. *Wildflowers of the Southeastern United States*. Athens: University of Georgia Press.

Eisel, M. T. 1977. *A Shoreline Survey: Great Peconic, Little Peconic, Gardiners and Napeague Bays*. Marine Science Center, State University of New York at Stonybrook, N.Y. Special Report No. 5 Reference 77-1.

Fassett, N. C. 1957. *A Manual of Aquatic Plants*. Madison: University of Wisconsin Press.

Fernald, M. L. 1950. *Gray's Manual of Botany*. 8th ed. New York: D. Van Nostrand.

Fisher, J. J. 1962. "Geomorphic Expression of Former Inlets along the Outer Banks of North Carolina." M.S. thesis. University of North Carolina, Chapel Hill.

Forman, R.T.T. 1979. *Pine Barrens: Ecosystem and Landscape*. New York: Academic Press.

Gemmel, A. R., Greig-Smith, P., and Giminghany, C. H. 1953. A Note on the Behavior of Ammophila Arenaria (L.) Link, in Relation to Sand Dune Formation. *Trans. Bot. Soc. Edin.* 35(2):132–36.

Gleason, H. A. 1952. *Illustrated Flora of the Northeastern United States and Adjacent Canada*. Vols. 1, 2, 3. Lancaster, Pa.: Lancaster Press.

Godfrey, P. J. 1976. Barrier Beaches of the East Coast. *Oceanic* 19(5):27–40.

Godfrey, P. J., and Godfrey; M. M. 1974. The Role of Overwash and Inlet Dynamics in the Formation of Salt Marshes on North Carolina Barrier Islands. In Reimold, R. J., and Queen, W. H., eds. *Ecology of Halophytes*. New York: Academic Press.

Godfrey, P. J., and Godfrey, M. M. 1976. Barrier Island Ecology of Cape Lookout National Seashore and Vicinity, North Carolina National Park Service Science Monograph No. 9.

Godfrey, R. K., and Wooten, J. W. 1979. *Aquatic and Wetland Plants of Southeastern United States. Monocotyledons*. Athens: University of Georgia Press.

Hitchcock, S. W. 1972. Fragile Nurseries of the Sea...Can We Save Our Salt Marshes? *National Geographic* 141:729–65.

Hosier, P. E. 1973. "The Effects of Oceanic Overwash on the Vegetation of Core and Shackelford Banks, N.C." Ph.D. dissertation. Duke University Durham, N.C.

Hotchkiss, N. 1970. *Common Marsh Plants of the United States and Canada*. Resource Publication 93. U.S. Fish & Wildlife Service, Department of the Interior, Washington, D.C.

Kearney, T. H. 1900. The Plant Covering of Ocracoke Island: A Study in the Ecology of North Carolina Strand Vegetation. *U.S. Herbarium Contributions* 5:261–319.

Martin, W. E. 1959. Vegetation of Island Beach State Park, N.J. *Ecological Monographs* 29:1–46.

Meanley, B. 1972. *Swamps, River Bottoms and Canebrakes*. Barre, Mass: Barre Publishers.

Niering, W. A. 1966. *The Life of the Marsh: North American Wetlands*. New York: McGraw-Hill.

Oosting, H. J. 1945. Tolerance to Salt Spray of Plants of Coastal Dunes. *Ecology* 26(1):85–89.

Oosting, H. J. 1954. Ecological Processes and Vegetation of the Maritime Strand in Southeastern United States. *Botanical Review* 20(4):226–62.

Oosting, H. J., and Billings, W. D. 1942. Factors Affecting Vegetational Zonation on Coastal Dunes. *Ecology* 23(2):133–42.

Petrides, G. A. 1972. *A Field Guide to Trees and Shrubs*. Boston: Houghton Mifflin.

Pierce, R. J. 1977. *Wetland Plants of the Eastern United States*. Army Corps of Engineers. New York.

Pilkey, O. H., Jr., Pilkey, O. H., Sr., and Turner, R. 1975. *How to Live with an Island*. N.C. Dept. of Natural & Economic Resources, Raleigh, N.C.

Queen, W. H. 1974. Physiology of Coastal Halophytes. In Reimold, R. J., and Queen, W. H., eds., *Ecology of Halophytes*. New York: Academic Press.

Radford, A. E., Ahles, H. E., and Bell, C. R. 1968. *Manual of Vascular Flora of the Carolinas*. Chapel Hill: University of North Carolina Press.

Redfield, A. 1972. Development of a New England Salt Marsh. *Ecological Monographs* 42(2).

Renshaw, C. 1969. The Beaches of Long Island. *Shore and Beach* 37(2): 50–69.

Saunders, C. F. 1900 *The Pine Barrens of New Jersey*. Proceedings of the Academy of Natural Science of Philadelphia, Part 3, pp. 544–49.

Sculthorpe, C. D. 1967. *The Biology of Aquatic Vascular Plants*. London: E. Arnold.

Settle, F. H. 1969. "Survey and Analysis of Changes Effected by Man on Tidal Wetlands of Virginia, 1955–1969." M.S. thesis. Virginia Polytechnic Institute and State University, Blacksburg, Va.

Shepard, F. P., and Wanless, H. R. 1971. *Our Changing Coastlines*. New York: McGraw-Hill.

Silberhorn, G. M. 1976. *Tidal Wetland Plants of Virginia*. Virginia Institute of Marine Science, Educational Series No. 19 Gloucester Point, Va.

Silberhorn, G. M., and Hennigar, H. F. 1981. Fire Island Foredune Ecology Study. Contract No. DACW72-80-C-0019. Dept. of the Army, Coastal Engineering Research Center, Fort Belvoir, Va.

Sutton, J. et al. 1980. *Wildflowers of the Outer Banks, Kitty Hawk to Hatteras*. Chapel Hill: University of North Carolina Press.

Taylor, N. 1923. *The Vegetation of Long Island, Part 1, The Vegetation of Montauk: A Study of Grassland and Forest*. Brooklyn Botanic Garden. Vol. 2, Brooklyn, N.Y.

Teal, J. M., and Teal, M. 1969. *Life and Death of the Salt Marsh*. Boston: Little, Brown.

Van der Walb, A. G. 1975. The Floristic Composition and Structure of Foredune Plant Communities on Cape Hatteras National Seashore. *Chesapeake Science* 16(2):115–26.

Wagner, R. H. 1964. The Ecology of *Uniola paniculata* in the Dunestrand Habitat of North Carolina. *Ecological Monographs* 34(1):79–96.

Welch, W. L. 1886. Opening Hatteras Inlet. *Bulletin of the Essex Institute* 17:37–42.

Wells, B. W. 1928. Plant Communities of the Coastal Plain of North Carolina and their Successional Relations. *Ecology* 9(2):230–43.

Wells, B. W., and Shunk, I. V. 1938. Salt Spray: An Important Factor in Coastal Ecology. *Bulletin of the Torrey Botanical Club* 65:485–92.

Index